"*Raising Prophetic Kids* is a n
as they partner with God in ra
time when today's youth face unprecedented challenges, Debra
Giles shares practical tools to ensure children thrive spiritually
and fulfill their God-given destiny."

Charlene Aaron, television co-host and news anchor, CBN

"This book is truly amazing! With five gifted sons of my own, I
can attest to its phenomenal principles for parenting. Whether
you're aware of having prophetic children or not, the guidelines
and instructions are invaluable. Thanks for sharing your trans-
parent journey, Apostle Debra!"

Prophetess Brenda Todd, Gap Standers International

"To see and hear the profound ministry of Apostle Debra Giles
is to experience the intense background of warfare, worship,
and tutelage of this esteemed author. She's more than qualified to show you how to activate a prophetic child, believe their
experiences, cultivate environments for growth and discovery,
become a helper in their destiny, build a sturdy foundation,
teach them balance, and show them how to live in legacy! This
prophet knows when to let go and when to hold fast. All of
these are principles that must be established to raise a successful
child of the prophetic. If you'd never met the author but saw
the product in her children, you would have to admit beyond
the shadow of a doubt that she is a success. If you follow the
principles herein, the results are certain to make you weep with
gladness but also pray with faith and become a skillful parent
of sagacious children. Superb job, my sister, inside the pages
of the book and in real life."

Apostle Pam Vinnett, Pam Vinnett Ministries

RAISING PROPHETIC KIDS

THE BUILDING BLOCKS
OF NURTURING
SPIRITUAL GIFTS

DEBRA GILES

Chosen

a division of Baker Publishing Group
Minneapolis, Minnesota

Published by Chosen Books
Minneapolis, Minnesota
ChosenBooks.com

Chosen Books is a division of
Baker Publishing Group, Grand Rapids, Michigan
Printed in the United States of America

Library of Congress Cataloging-in-Publication Data
Names: Giles, Debra, author.
Title: Raising prophetic kids : the building blocks of nurturing spiritual gifts / Debra Giles.
Description: Minneapolis, Minnesota : Chosen Books, a division of Baker Publishing Group, [2024] | Includes bibliographical references.
Identifiers: LCCN 2023048330 | ISBN 9780800772499 (paper) | ISBN 9780800772536 (casebound) | ISBN 9781493445646 (ebook)
Subjects: LCSH: Child rearing—Religious aspects—Christianity. | Parenting—Religious aspects—Christianity. | Gifts, Spiritual. | Prophecy.
Classification: LCC BV4529 .G553 2024 | DDC 248.8/45—dc23/eng/20231205
LC record available at https://lccn.loc.gov/2023048330

Unless otherwise indicated, Scripture quotations are from the Berean Bible (www.Berean.Bible), Berean Study Bible (BSB) © 2016–2020 by Bible Hub and Berean.Bible. Used by permission. All rights reserved.

Scripture identified AMP taken from the Amplified Bible, Copyright © 1954, 1958, 1962, 1964, 1965, 1987 by The Lockman Foundation. Used by permission.

Scripture quotations identified CEV are from the Contemporary English Version © 1991, 1992, 1995 by American Bible Society. Used by permission.

Scripture quotations identified ESV are from The Holy Bible, English Standard Version® (ESV®), copyright © 2001 by Crossway, a publishing ministry of Good News Publishers. Used by permission. All rights reserved. ESV Text Edition: 2016

Scripture quotations identified GNT are from the Good News Translation in Today's English Version-Second Edition. Copyright © 1992 by American Bible Society. Used by permission.

Scripture quotations identified HCSB are from the Holman Christian Standard Bible®, copyright © 1999, 2000, 2002, 2003, 2009 by Holman Bible Publishers. Used by permission. Holman Christian Standard Bible®, Holman CSB®, and HCSB® are federally registered trademarks of Holman Bible Publishers.

Scripture quotations marked LEB are from the Lexham English Bible. Copyright 2012 Logos Bible Software. Lexham is a registered trademark of Logos Bible Software.

Scripture quotations identified MSG are taken from The Message, copyright © 1993, 2002, 2018 by Eugene H. Peterson. Used by permission of NavPress. All rights reserved. Represented by Tyndale House Publishers.

Scriptures identified NIV taken from the Holy Bible, New International Version®, NIV®. Copyright © 1973, 1978, 1984, 2011 by Biblica, Inc.® Used by permission of Zondervan. All rights reserved worldwide. www.zondervan.com. The "NIV" and "New International Version" are trademarks registered in the United States Patent and Trademark Office by Biblica, Inc.®

Scripture identified NKJV taken from the New King James Version®. Copyright © 1982 by Thomas Nelson. Used by permission. All rights reserved.

Scripture quotations identified NLT are taken from the Holy Bible, New Living Translation, copyright © 1996, 2004, 2015 by Tyndale House Foundation. Used by permission of Tyndale House Publishers, Carol Stream, Illinois 60188. All rights reserved.

Cover design by Rob Williams
Cover images from Shutterstock

Author is represented by the literary agency of Embolden Media Group, LLC.

Baker Publishing Group publications use paper produced from sustainable forestry practices and postconsumer waste whenever possible.

24 25 26 27 28 29 30   7 6 5 4 3 2 1

To my granddaughter and those
who in generations to come will need assistance
to grow and develop their prophetic gifts.

CONTENTS

FOREWORD

Apostle Debra Giles's detailed account of prophetically nurturing her four boys left me nearly speechless. Before reading her book, I'd never come across anything even remotely close to her insights into raising prophetic children, nor was I aware that such insights into raising prophetic children existed.

Apostle Debra made me reflect on my four grown children and the pivotal period I overlooked in nurturing their spiritual abilities because I assumed they were too young. Take, for instance, my youngest daughter, who as a toddler saw things none of us could see and had extraordinary dreams. If I'd had access to the insights Apostle Debra provides in her book, I am convinced my daughter would have flourished even more in her God-given gifts.

At the age of twenty-three, when I welcomed my first child, my focus in preparing for her arrival revolved around buying the crib, bottles, and diapers. The concept of prophetically training an infant wasn't on my radar. Apostle Debra's teachings shed light on cultivating a prophetic environment for your baby, going beyond nursery preparation.

Apostle Debra delves deeper, guiding parents on how to nurture their children's gifts even while they're in the womb. Yes, you read that right! While your children are still in utero, as a parent or grandparent you can initiate prophetic nurturing and impart teachings to your child or grandchild. Moreover, she will teach you how to establish a routine of prayer and Scripture memorization for toddlers, and she offers insights into prophetically parenting adolescents.

Each of my four grown children was brought up in a home steeped in faith, and they've all achieved success without causing me a moment's worry. I'm truly proud that they've upheld their devotion to the Lord. But I can't help but contemplate how different the course of their lives might have been if I'd had Apostle Debra's book when my children experienced the trauma of losing their father at such tender ages. Regrettably, children often endure traumatic events that linger into their adult years. Apostle Debra, mindful of parents with grown children, also equips us with tools to persist in nurturing our adult offspring.

Within the chapters of *Raising Prophetic Kids*, Apostle Debra's uncanny and prolific teaching reveals easy-to-understand keys on fostering prophetic sensibilities in children, nurturing their spiritual growth, and empowering them to embrace their unique gifts. She underscores the profound responsibility parents have in shaping a child's journey. By recognizing and supporting children's inherent talents and inclinations, parents then become facilitators in guiding children toward fulfilling their prophetic assignment.

Raising Prophetic Kids exceeded my expectations. Apostle Debra's teaching style is a blend of the biblical, technical, and even scientific realms. She adeptly weaves together biblical principles and laws with insights from psychology, biology, and a comprehensive understanding of the supernatural aspects of the spirit world.

I firmly believe that *Raising Prophetic Kids* will become the go-to resource for parents, counselors, and ministries not just in our nation but globally. This book serves as a crucial tool for families aiming to establish a lasting, divine legacy for generations to come.

Pastor Riva Tims Watkins

INTRODUCTION

Think back to before your child was born, to when you were filled with wonder and imagined what their personality would be and who they would become. It's common for parents-to-be to daydream about their little bundle of joy waiting to be born, anticipating their future accomplishments and envisioning their character traits. Fathers often purchase trinkets that represent their favorite sport or another interest they hope to share with their son or daughter. Mothers might place sentimental items into a hope chest, start a scrapbook for the baby, or ready a nursery.

Preparing for our kids' arrival and providing material things for them is good. It's even more important, however, to prepare and provide for them spiritually. As their parents, we're responsible to teach them how to discern between good and evil and live a life pleasing to God. We're also responsible for teaching them how to protect and defend themselves with spiritual armor—learning God's Word and how to pray, speak prophetic declarations, and contend for the manifestation of the prophetic words spoken over them.

Your praying over your kids and speaking life to them are two of your main tasks. These are types of prophetic guidance God gives you authority to exercise in their lives, as the prophetic is all about communication with Him—hearing His voice, obeying what we hear, and responding to His leading. And as we'll soon discover, our prophetic guidance continues long after our kids are born and as long as the Lord allows us to help prepare them for their purpose here on earth.

I am a prophet, teacher, and mother who raised four incredible, prophetic sons. From the time they were in the cradle, I sought God's wisdom for how to guide them into the paths they should take. He provided for me a beneficial approach to help them become their best selves even as little humans with a godly imprint. He gave me insight into their personalities and led me in how to nurture what they were meant to be. And as they grew, I discovered seeds of greatness in them that needed cultivation, including spiritual sensitivity and both natural and spiritual gifting.

While they're young, it's important to teach kids to focus on living godly principles, so teaching my sons how to pray, hear God for themselves, and develop their own prayer lives was essential. I often scheduled Bible story time or Scripture reading and prayer before naps. But, of course, the strategies for encouraging them in their spiritual lives changed as they grew. I continue to speak into their lives as adults today, but I do it less often as they each implement what they learned from me, walk out their God-given purpose, and embrace their prophetic gifts.

Perhaps your daughter has come to you about a dream or feeling she's had about some future happening. Maybe during prayer or worship your son has seen angels or blurted some message you know could have come only from the Lord. Or maybe you're not a parent yet, but you want to prepare a spiritually rich environment into which your future child can be born so they'll have every opportunity to become whoever God has uniquely fashioned them to be.

Whatever your current situation, I've written this book for you. I've shared the Bible-based strategies and building blocks I learned for nurturing children's spiritual gifts, beginning with creating a spiritually rich environment to draw out and develop the prophetic in them throughout the various stages of their lives and in preparation for a lifetime of service to and relationship with God. In addition, at the end of each chapter you'll find a prophetic activity you can do to enhance your experience.

Parents, we can help prepare the next generation—the young Samuels, Davids, Deborahs, Issachars, and Elishas of our day who will worship the Lord wholeheartedly, speak the word for such a time as this, and help navigate the church through perilous times and seasons. Just as Hannah, Elizabeth, and Mary were called to raise sons whose prophetic voices changed the world, you are called to usher your son or daughter into their own high calling.

If you're ready to partner with God to raise kids to whom He speaks and shares His secrets, turn the page, and let's begin.

Cultivating a Spiritually Rich Environment

At the age of fourteen, years before my parents decided to serve God, I became a Christian. I was born again. Until then, I'd attended church only occasionally with my great-aunt, maternal grandmother, or a friend. Still, I'd become acquainted with a place of worship where the gifts of the Spirit flowed, and great emphasis was placed on having faith and knowing and exercising your authority in Christ. I joined that church and began to grow spiritually.

After learning about passed-down patterns of negative behavior that can be attributed to generational curses, I decided to reverse the curses I'd identified in my own bloodline (more about how to do this in a later chapter). I wanted to pass down my faith and new life to my kids when I married and started a family. I wanted to raise my kids in the nurture and admonition of the Lord and release generational blessings instead of curses. I wanted to be intentional about shaping their future and exposing them to the things of God. My job as their mother would be to not only take them to church but to teach them at home.

Growing up, I'd always wanted two kids—a boy and a girl. But God had other plans. When I married, He blessed me with four sons who were all future leaders, giving me the privilege of pouring into them. Let me tell you a little about each one.

My Four Sons

My oldest son is a quiet storm, laid-back, and quite the philosopher. He loves nature and animals, and I'm not surprised by that. While he was still in the womb, I held my belly during our bonding times and introduced him to the outside world he'd see once he was born. I described majestic trees, green grass, beautiful flowers, mountains, and so much more of God's creation.

Along with his younger brothers, he suffered from asthma, and after an attack he would have to stay home from school to recuperate. Sometimes he couldn't even run and play like other kids, but I observed his resilience and faith as he navigated those limitations. Then one day when he was watching a healing evangelist on television, he laid his hands on the screen during prayer and was healed. His health improved from that time on.

This son is musically inclined and sings and plays drums. He also started having prophetic dreams around age four or five. Most of his dreams are literal, meaning he sees real-life events before they happen. He's a seer.

My second son, also musically gifted, is known for singing and leading worship. He loves to cook and build things. He's adventurous and loves the outdoors. Growing up, he was often outside catching grasshoppers and other insects.

When this son was a toddler, my dad brought to my attention that he would stop what he was doing around a certain time every day and praise God. At eight years old, he was filled with the Spirit during a church conference. A few years later, one day he started playing the keyboard as he sang in worship. His dad and I were stunned because he'd never had lessons, and we'd had no idea he could play. He picked up playing drums as well. Today he writes and sings prophetic songs.

Son number three, who is quite like my oldest son, loves sports, especially basketball. I knew he would play ball when he reached for the photographer's ball at three months old during a photo shoot. As he grew older, I cultivated that natural gift by teaching him how to dribble, throw, and pass. He's gifted to play the keyboard and drums and to sing.

He is also a seer. God will sometimes show him things before they happen too. Around age seven, he had an open-eye vision of one of his god-brothers getting into trouble with law enforcement. A few weeks later, exactly what he saw happened. (I'll describe what an open-eye vision is in chapter 4.)

My youngest son, Josh, is a global minister, conference speaker, singer, and prolific author. He wanted to be a writer starting in elementary school, where he had the opportunity to write his first book through a journalism program. He's a dreamer and a prophet, prophesying after the anointing came on him at a young age. He was wise beyond his years, and it's evident today as he impacts thousands with his revelatory teachings.

During their formative years, my sons formed a singing group called The Giles Brothers and sang for family at special occasions and at church. They wrote their own songs and sang a capella until they learned to play instruments well enough to accompany themselves.

As they grew, they each also developed their own prayer life. One Saturday morning, I came downstairs to hear them all praying. One of them had awakened early and slipped downstairs to pray. Soon, one by one, they all woke up and came down to join in. They weren't prompted by me or anyone else; they were sensitive to the Holy Spirit and prayed on their own.

Children and the Prophetic Dimension

Since young children are newly born from eternity, they're more sensitive to the supernatural realm. Kids may see or hear what adults do not, similar to the sensitivity an animal may have to sights and sounds not seen or heard by humans. This often allows them to be open to the prophetic dimension (also known as the heavenly realm), a place in the spirit realm where God gives access to the future through the gifts of the Spirit—namely, dreams, visions, prophecy, and discernment. In chapter 4, we'll talk about dreams, visions, and prophecy in detail, and you'll see evidence of the gift of discernment in many of the Scriptures and stories from the Bible I share.

The purpose for the Lord's giving access to the prophetic dimension, which taps into His mind and heart, is to foretell the future and bring glory to Him in doing so. Amos 3:7 declares God's special relationship with those who open themselves to knowing the secrets in His mind and on His heart: "Surely my Lord does not do anything unless he has revealed his secret to his servants the prophets" (LEB).

Immersed in the prophetic dimension, I had dreams and visions as a young child. But my parents did not seem to understand them or my prophetic gifts, so I stopped sharing these experiences with them. My maternal grandmother, however, always seemed interested when I went to her with something new to share. She never interpreted my dreams, but providing a listening ear was enough. Since someone I looked up to was willing to take the time to hear what I had to say and, I felt, validate my experiences, I was okay.

Then when I was a young believer in the 1970s, not much emphasis was placed on the prophetic dimension in churches.

So although I continued to have dreams and divine encounters, I had little guidance. That's when I decided to cultivate a spiritually rich environment in my own home and other places as God led and share what I learned with my future children and others.

In this chapter, we'll first consider what you can do as a parent to cultivate a spiritually rich environment even before your child is born. And then we'll discuss what you can do as your child progresses through early childhood, adolescence, and even into adulthood. No matter where you are on your parenting journey, it's never too soon or too late to start establishing what you need to support and walk alongside your prophetic child.

Before Your Child Is Born

We all existed in the mind of the Lord before we were created and born in human form. God's plans for each of us are sure, and the details of those plans are infused in our DNA. God confirmed His plans for Jeremiah by assuring him that He already knew what he would become because He'd meticulously planned it. He says to him in Jeremiah 1:5, "Before I formed you in the womb I knew you, and before you came from the womb I consecrated you; I appointed you as a prophet to the nations" (LEB).

God does the same for our kids even before they're born. And so—mom, dad, or caregiver—you must seek Him to unlock your child's purpose and receive insight into their giftings and callings just as you must seek Him for your own. This will help you speak over them effectively and call into being what begins in seed form.

Following are three steps you can take to create a spiritually rich environment for your child even before they enter this world.

1. Speak life

One of the most profound ways you can pour into your child is through what you speak, how you speak, and what you allow them to hear even while they're still in utero. Science has acknowledged that unborn babies can hear the outside world. One medically reviewed article says, "Around week 25 or 26, babies in the womb have been shown to respond to voices and noise."[1]

This confirms what we know from Scripture. One day Elizabeth, who was carrying John the Baptist, was visited by Mary, who was carrying Jesus. Luke 1:41 tells us, "When Elizabeth heard the greeting of Mary, the baby in her womb leaped" (LEB). This passage reveals that the unborn can respond to what they hear and express emotion.

And because the unborn can hear, parents must be careful about what they say—even about their child. Proverbs 18:21 tells us, "What you say can preserve life or destroy it" (GNT). That's true for a child's well-being even before birth, so speak positive affirmations. Sing and play positive music. Control what sounds your unborn baby hears the best you can. And never argue.

With every pregnancy, I not only sang to and read Scripture for the child I was carrying but also prayed over the baby, interceding for his health and development. And every day I spoke to my womb, prophesying that God would use my child for His glory. I prophesied that the blessings of the Lord would follow him throughout his life.

This takes me back to the story about unborn sons John the Baptist and Jesus. Filled with the Holy Spirit, Elizabeth then prophesied and released blessings on Mary and her unborn child. During their conversation, each woman excitedly responded to the privilege of carrying a child with great purpose. This and many other experiences I share throughout this book reveal that it's a parent's task to guard and protect the preciousness of what they've conceived.

The enemy will often try to keep children from fully developing and being birthed to fulfill their God-ordained purpose. This is a truth I experienced firsthand. When I was pregnant with my first son, my doctor told me I might have complications during delivery because I was so small. He didn't know if I would be able to give birth to my baby naturally. I sensed the enemy wanted to interrupt God's plan, so I prayed over my child for a smooth delivery. God is good. My son was born healthy with no problems during the birth.

Don't wait until your child is born to pray and prophesy over them. Do it while they're still in the womb. The devil is a liar, and he wants to thwart God's plan at every turn. Ask God for specific prayers for each child. Pray for His will to be done on earth and in your child's life as it is in heaven, and know that God is faithful to carry out the fullness of His plan for every child He creates.

2. Break generational curses

One night when I was pregnant with my second son, during a church service, my stomach began to hurt as I prayed to break generational curses. At that moment I knew the child I carried had great purpose and that the enemy would try to stop God's plans. When the time came for his delivery, my baby almost went into fetal distress. But thank God, he was born healthy. I spoke declarations over his life that the Lord would use him for His glory and that he would love and honor God throughout his life.

While in prayer to break generational curses, you may come up against demonic spirits. Demonic entities are assigned—even from birth—to hinder us, to wreak havoc in our lives, and to attempt to destroy us. Jesus identified Satan's overall assignment against mankind during one of His teachings: "The thief comes only to steal and kill and destroy" (John 10:10). Further illustration of how the enemy can seek to snuff out our purpose even from birth is King Herod's attempt to track the baby Jesus so he could kill Him. An angel told Joseph in a dream, "Take the Child and His mother and flee to Egypt. Stay there until I tell you, for Herod is going to search for the Child to kill Him" (Matthew 2:13).

But then guardian angels are assigned to us at birth. Jesus said, "See that you do not look down on any of these little ones. For I tell you that their angels in heaven always see the face of My Father in heaven" (Matthew 18:10). These angelic guardians are responsible to protect us against evil and anything meant to harm: "No evil will conquer you; no plague will come near your home. For he will order his angels to protect you wherever you go" (Psalm 91:10–11 NLT). Hebrews 1:14 also confirms that God sends angels to help humans: "Angels are only servants— spirits sent to care for people who will inherit salvation" (NLT).

Don't be afraid to pray to break the strongholds in your bloodline even before you have kids. When you do, you're bringing deliverance to your future seed. Strongholds are demonic spirits that have attached themselves through openings in the soul. They wait for times of vulnerability brought about through trauma, rejection, or abandonment, so they may have been there a long time. They wait patiently, even for decades, to take advantage, and they often work in conjunction with other spirits to fortify themselves. They look for spirits even more evil than themselves to accompany and become spiritual hosts in the soul of their victim:

> When an impure spirit comes out of a person, it goes through arid places seeking rest and does not find it. Then it says, "I will return to the house I left." When it arrives, it finds the house unoccupied, swept clean and put in order. Then it goes and takes with it seven other spirits more wicked than itself, and they go in and live there. And the final condition of that person is worse than the first.
>
> Matthew 12:43–45 NIV

In Matthew 12:29, Jesus says, "How can someone enter into the house of a strong man and steal his property, unless he first ties up the strong man?" (LEB). The strong man must be bound in order to be free and get rid of the others that have also attached themselves to a person's soul. The strong man is not the most wicked demonic spirit but the one who knows the vulnerabilities of the person and how to enter their soul.

This Scripture can be used to describe how the root spirit enters into the soul and brings other more wicked spirits to fortify itself to keep from being cast out. Unless the root spirit is identified and dealt with, the person remains bound. For example, it can be said that a person addicted to alcohol will be okay if they just stop drinking. But drinking is usually just a symptom that hides the root cause of why the person drinks. If the root is identified and dealt with, then the spirits who have fortified it can be dealt with.

The process toward spiritual deliverance involves casting out demons, being healed, and closing doors that may have been opened during a traumatic event. These doors can be opened without the consent of the victim. For instance, someone who was molested may have issues with others who are the gender and age of the molester. They may also fight with spirits associated with the trauma, such as lust, depression, suicidal thoughts, rejection, low self-esteem, and a lack of self-love.

The enemy is the culprit behind this. He sows seeds and then goes away for a season before returning to see if his seeds have taken root. This is what happens when a traumatic experience takes place. The enemy hopes demonic seeds will be planted and grow. Jesus told a parable that relates to this: "While men slept, his enemy came and sowed tares among the wheat and went his way. . . . He said to them, 'An enemy has done this'" (Matthew 13:25, 28 NKJV).

Again, don't be afraid to ask God to break the strongholds in your bloodline even before your child is born—and certainly after they're born if you become newly aware of strongholds in your family's history or present.

3. Remain strong in faith

I was shocked to learn that my third son was in a breech position. My pregnancy had been going well, and I'd had no indication that anything was out of the ordinary. We had a few months to go before his birth, and we prayed that he would turn on his own. God honored our prayers, and our baby turned into the proper birth position after a short time. I believe that God's answer to our prayer activated the change in our son's position, and he was born with no complications.

Sometimes when things are going well, the enemy brings up obstacles. Be consistent and confident that through the power of prayer you will overcome whatever comes your way. You already have the victory because you fight from the place of victory.

Encouragement in times of challenges

Maybe you have had difficulty in childbearing. Maybe you've lost a child or are in a situation where you are separated from children. I want to give you some encouragement. Although I am writing this book from my parenting perspective and experiences, I want you to know that as a minister, I am sensitive to your experiences too and have prayed with many families in various situations. God has a plan for each of us and our children. My prayer is that He will bring you comfort and hope in knowing that His goodness toward you supersedes any circumstance you and your family face. He is our helper in difficult times and gives us wisdom and strength to navigate all that happens to us. As Psalm 46:1 (MSG) says, "God is a safe place to hide, ready to help when we need him.

I pray that, even as we all have different experiences raising children, He will use our stories as testaments of His glory, love, and goodness. And that wherever you have had times of sadness and vulnerability, He will comfort you by encompassing you in His agape love and showering you with joy.

During the pregnancy with my fourth son, I was so sick one day that I thought I was literally going to die. I'd never had morning sickness, and this definitely made up for every other pregnancy. I couldn't eat or drink anything. I had no strength. I couldn't even lift my arm, and my mom had to bathe me. At first, I thought this illness might be the stomach flu, but it lasted only one day and then I was back to normal. This was another indication that the enemy wanted to interrupt God's plan.

I knew I had to war and speak life over my unborn sons as I sensed seeds of greatness in each of them. I was determined to never allow the enemy to make me believe that I would not bring my babies to full term and deliver them healthy. I released prophetic decrees over them according to Job 22:28: "You will also declare a thing, and it will be established for you" (NKJV).

The King James Version of the Bible uses the word *decree* as a verb rather than the verb *declare* found in other versions and translations. I've chosen to use both when it comes to speaking declarations, as the words have slightly different meanings yet they're both important to our not only having authority in Christ but being firm in it:

> Decree is a noun that means an official order issued by a legal authority. It can also be used as a verb to mean to issue such an order. . . . Declare, on the other hand, is a verb that means to announce or make known publicly. It can also mean to state something firmly or emphatically.[2]

Here are declarations to speak over your unborn child:

I decree and declare that you will be carried to full term.

I decree and declare that you will be born healthy.

25

I decree and declare that you will love God with all your heart.

I decree and declare that you will understand and embrace your purpose.

Here are declarations to speak over yourself as a parent:

I decree and declare that I will nurture this child and pour into them the things of God.

I decree and declare that I will be a godly example for my child.

After Your Child Is Born

Here are three ways you can continue cultivating a spiritually rich and prophetic environment after your child is born.

1. Protect your child from harm

You must now protect your child outside of the womb and ensure they can grow and develop both naturally and spiritually in a safe environment.

As mentioned earlier, an angel spoke to Joseph, Jesus' earthly father, in a dream: "'Get up,' he said, 'take the child and his mother and escape to Egypt. Stay there until I tell you, for Herod is going to search for the child to kill him'" (Matthew 2:13). Joseph had a prophetic dream of warning that instructed him how to keep Jesus safe, and he took the warning seriously and moved his family geographically.

The dream was also urgent and time sensitive. Had Joseph waited, it would have jeopardized the life of our Savior and altered His earthly assignment. The move provided time for Jesus to continue growing and developing.

Perhaps God hasn't spoken to you to this extreme, but if it means protecting your child, He can and He will. Continually speak the following declaration over your child: *I decree and declare that the angels of the Lord will protect my child day and night.*

2. Nurture your child's gifts

As your child grows, observe their gifts and talents as well as any unusual ways God deals with them. *Merriam-Webster's* dictionary defines a gift as "a notable capacity, talent, or endowment."[3] Look for what comes naturally to your child even though they didn't learn it or study it or should even be capable of achieving it.

Nurturing goes beyond making sure we feed, change, and bathe newborns. Pour into your child the things of God and speak to them about their purpose as God reveals details to you.

Let's look at a few types of both spiritual and natural gifts you may observe and then nurture in your son or daughter.

Types of spiritual gifts:

- prophetic (dreams, visions, prophecy, discernment)
- wisdom beyond years
- prophetic arts (expressing worship through liturgical dance, song, playing instruments, spoken word, poems)
- compassion (exhibits a desire to assist others in an uncommon way)

Types of natural gifts:

- musically inclined (can sing or play instruments)
- intelligence beyond expected age
- athletic

- creative (inventive; imaginative; artistic; writes, tells, or acts out stories)
- mechanically inclined (repairs, assembles, or breaks down items to see how they work)

3. Prepare your child for their purpose

One of the most valuable things you can do for your child is to teach them in preparation for their purpose on earth. Hannah prayed for a son, making a Nazarite vow similar to the one Samson's parents made:

> LORD Almighty, look at me, your servant! See my trouble and remember me! Don't forget me! If you give me a son, I promise that I will dedicate him to you for his whole life and that he will never have his hair cut.
>
> 1 Samuel 1:11 GNT

God answered her prayer, and Hannah kept her vow and prepared Samuel for his purpose. She nurtured him until he was ready for the first phase of that purpose, ministering in the temple. Then she took him to Eli the priest so he could train him in how to minister to God. Samuel went on to become a renowned prophet God used to anoint and advise kings. He accomplished every God-given assignment and walked in the integrity of his parents, Hannah and Elkanah, despite the sinful behavior he saw from Eli's sons, Hophni and Phinehas, whom the priest had also trained.

I can imagine little Samuel curiously asking his mother why he would soon live in the temple, and Hannah sharing how she prayed and offered him to God. She must have moved according to divine instructions and God's timing, because she didn't take him there until he was weaned. But she continued to keep her vow:

28

I am the woman who was standing here in your presence, praying to the LORD. For this child I prayed, and the Lord has granted me my petition that I made to him. Therefore I have lent him to the LORD. As long as he lives, he is lent to the LORD.

1 Samuel 1:26–28 ESV

She also continued nurturing Samuel after he'd left home. Every year she made a new coat for him and took it to him.

Next let's consider how you can cultivate what your child needs from you in each of these stages of life: early childhood, adolescence, and adulthood. I also provide more declarations you can speak over your child at each stage.

Early Childhood

Establish a routine

Even when your child is as young as a toddler, it's essential to instill godly values and principles. Start and end each day with prayer—and include your young child in other times of prayer as well. Share Bible stories with them. Teaching kids the Bible at a young age provides a good spiritual foundation. You can start by teaching them the psalms. Some may say this stage is too young, but I beg to differ. Notice kids still in diapers recognizing music, singing a specific song, or having a favorite TV show, character, or commercial.

My youngest three children learned all of Psalm 100 while they were toddlers. They attended Christian school at the time, and the principal believed in exposing all the students to the same Scriptures during chapel no matter their age. It was noted that the younger kids learned this psalm quicker than the older ones did. (My youngest was only two, y'all.)

It's never too late to establish a spiritually rich routine with your child in early childhood, from toddler to preteen.

Watch your words

Parents help shape little souls with personalities and emotions who will make mistakes and grow from them just like we did and still do. Once I heard a mother scold her daughter, who was around the age of four. Afterward, she commented that the girl knew better than to do what she'd done. I reminded her that this little one was still learning on this journey called life as she had been on earth for only a short time.

Sometimes we adults expect too much too soon from kids, forgetting that we, too, make mistakes and are still learning ourselves. We must remember to extend grace to them, because we expect it to be extended to us. It's essential to carefully craft words spoken over your child even when you're disappointed by or upset with them. There will be times of discipline, yes, but even then your words can cause a lasting negative effect if spoken too harshly. Encouraging words go a long way in a better direction.

Cultivate the seeds

I often say there are seeds of greatness in everyone, and those seeds must be cultivated and developed. If allowed to blossom, who knows what your child may become? A great president? An inventor? The next Einstein? Who knows?

An article about brain development in young kids tells us, "Children's brains develop in spurts called critical periods. The first occurs around age 2, with a second one occurring during adolescence." The article goes on to discuss how the parents of genius Albert Einstein consulted a doctor because he seemed to have a severe delay in language development. His parents didn't give up on him but found a way to help stimulate and unlock this delay in his development. When he was around the age of five, his mother, gifted in music herself, gave him a violin, and his father gave him a compass. "These two gifts challenged Einstein's brain in distinctive ways at just the right time." [4]

Though a little late, Einstein's process began within the critical phase of development between ages two and seven. As referred to previously,

> This first critical period of brain development begins around age 2 and concludes around age 7. It provides a prime opportunity to lay the foundation for a holistic education for children. [5]

Watch and see

I encourage you not only to dedicate your child to God but to ask Him how you should pray for them, what He has planned for them, and what special ways you can align your parenting with His plans. After doing this, write down what God reveals to you and date each item so you can track them. Then follow His instructions and keep praying for the will of God to come to pass. It won't happen overnight, but you will see new things as your kids grow and develop even into adolescence and adulthood.

Here are declarations to speak over your young child:

I decree and declare that you will grow and develop in the word and will of God.

I decree and declare that you will love God with your whole heart.

I decree and declare that you will walk in your purpose on the earth.

I decree and declare that you will be taught about Jesus and the kingdom of God.

I decree and declare that you have seeds of greatness and that they will be developed.

Adolescence

Don't stop now

Adolescence is a time of discovery and inquisitiveness. The body and mind are still developing, so this is no time for parents to pull back from investing in their child's spiritual growth. Of course, there may be new challenges since your child has gained independence in so many areas. But continue to nurture them—naturally and spiritually—and cultivate the gifts you've seen as well as what God may have shown you still in seed form.

By now your child should have developed a prayer life and started reading the Bible without being prompted to do so. If there's resistance in these areas, ask God to show you how to pray for them and to give you wisdom on how and when to speak to them about it. Be sure not to nag them, though. That will only push them further away from the things of God. But it's good to still have family prayer times that include their participation.

Stick to your core values

As they grow, more and more your child will encounter the outside world that doesn't look like the environment you've established at home. They may be influenced by friends who don't have the same core values in which you're raising them. Ephesians 6:4 instructs us in this, starting with our approach: "Parents, don't be hard on your children. Raise them properly. Teach them and instruct them about the Lord" (CEV).

It's our job as parents to give our child a strong foundation, but they have to choose to continue walking in what they've learned. The Bible says that if we teach them, the teachings will not leave them: "Teach your children right from wrong, and when they are grown they will still do right" (Proverbs 22:6 CEV).

Be a good example

I still think about many things my parents taught me as I was growing up. From my mother I learned to be compassionate and kind. If she was out driving and saw anyone she knew walking along, she'd stop and ask if they needed a ride. I've found myself doing the same. I often ask God to never let me lose my compassion, especially if I sense my heart is becoming cold.

It's easy to focus on our own world and block out everything and everyone else. But with God's help, we can fight against that pull and be a good example to our child into their teen years and beyond.

Here are declarations to speak over your teen:

I decree and declare that you will continue to grow and develop in the word and will of God.

I decree and declare that you will continue to love God with your whole heart.

I decree and declare that you will not derail your purpose on the earth.

I decree and declare that you will make positive choices.

Adulthood

We'll talk much more about adult children in the chapter about letting go, but here let's cover three principles that will help you continue cultivating a spiritually rich environment for your child who's grown up and become independent.

Never turn your back

Watching your child enter adulthood can be scary, but knowing you've nurtured and poured into them, you now put them in God's hands. They will make mistakes just as you did and still do, so be gentle and loving, always embracing them no matter what. They may have to reap consequences as a result of their mistakes, but you can love them through it. Never turn your back on your child even if you have to exhibit tough love. God has never turned His back on us, and neither should we turn our backs on our children.

Become an advisor

When you know you've raised your child right, allow them the space to apply what they've learned as they enter adulthood. Take on the role of advisor, though still covering them in prayer and speaking over their life, asking God to bring His plan for them to pass.

Continue to speak and pray

War over the prophetic words God gives you for your adult child, and then keep praying until you see what He's said about those words operating in their life. Numbers 23:19 tells us, "God is not human, that he should lie, not a human being, that he should change his mind." If God said it, it *will* come to pass. But there is an appointed time and season for your child to walk in their destiny, because God's plan for them is intentional.

Mary pondered many things spoken about Jesus and kept them in her heart from the time the angel told her He would be great:

> He . . . will be called the Son of the Most High. The Lord God will give him the throne of his father David, and he will reign over Jacob's descendants forever; his kingdom will never end.
>
> Luke 1:30–33 NIV

We know Mary took this prophecy seriously, because she went to Jesus during a wedding and in so many words said, "The host is out of wine, and they will be embarrassed. Do something miraculous." She told the staff to follow His instructions and do whatever He said even though Jesus tried to convince her it wasn't time for Him to operate His gifts (John 2:1–5).

Again, there's an appointed time and season for us all to walk into our destiny, as confirmed in the lives of David and Jeremiah. In Psalm 139:16, David says to the Lord, "All the days ordained for me were written in your book before one of them came to be" (NIV). And as mentioned before, to Jeremiah God said, "Before you were born I set you apart and appointed you as a prophet to the nations" (Jeremiah 1:5).

Here are declarations to speak over your adult child:

I decree and declare that you will continue to walk in the ways of God.

I decree and declare that you will seek God for wisdom before making decisions.

I decree and declare that you will serve God all the days of your life.

I decree and declare that you will walk into your purpose.

If you work to implement what we've discussed in this chapter within your parenting style, your home, and your prayer life, you'll be actively participating with God in developing and releasing your child's prophetic purpose.

Now that you're aware of what helps create the right environment for your child's spiritual flourishing—whether you're about to start a family, waiting on your bundle of joy to arrive, or already have a child—practice becoming your child's destiny helper, even if they're now an adult.

PROPHETIC ACTIVITY

Help create the right spiritual environment for your son or daughter by choosing to speak prophetic declarations over them and pray for results.

- Choose a prophetic declaration that best fits your current status.
- Say the declaration out loud daily.
- Customize the declaration and your prayers as needed.
- Declare and pray until you see results and feel that specific declaration and prayer are no longer needed.

Becoming Your Child's Destiny Helper

In chapter 1, I pointed out that your child has a destiny and that there's an appointed time and season for them to walk into that destiny. As a parent, you can help your child prepare for that time and season, whenever it comes.

Two major aspects of becoming your child's destiny helper are explored in this chapter: first, the importance of what name you choose for your son or daughter, and second, how you can support your child in developing the seeds of greatness in them. The latter involves providing guidance, redirecting their behavior if necessary, and reassuring them with love.

Naming Your Child

Naming your child is a more significant process than you may know. Intentional naming, traditional naming, naming around events or circumstances, and God's own desires can all come into play.

Naming intentionally

From the beginning of time, a name has pronounced the purpose of the person or thing it identifies. God spoke into existence each thing He desired to create and called it by name. For example, Genesis 1:5 describes the naming of day and night: "God called the light Day, and the darkness he called Night" (ESV). *Yom*, the Hebrew word for day, provides illumination, and night—or *choshek* in Hebrew—brings obscurity. Each one functions by what they were named.

God appointed Adam to name every beast and fowl He'd created, training him to be intentional. Adam understood the assignment. He named each one appropriately according to their characteristics. Giraffes, for example, cannot be mistaken for monkeys as their appearance and characteristics are distinctly different. Then Adam went on to name his wife, the woman presented to him from his own rib:

> Out of the ground the LORD God formed every beast of the field and every bird of the air, and brought them to Adam to see what he would call them. And whatever Adam called each living creature, that was its name. . . . Adam called his wife's name Eve, because she was the mother of all living.
>
> Genesis 2:19; 3:20 NKJV

Intentional naming can have personal benefits. For instance, simple, more common names often relate to higher ranks in careers.[1] And in an article that confirms that a child's name can affect their personality as well as how others see them, Professor David Zhu at Arizona State University is quoted as saying, "Because a name is used to identify an individual and communicate with the individual on a daily basis, it serves as the very basis of one's self-conception."[2]

Another article says,

It has long been known that grade-school children with highly unusual names or names with negative associations tend to be less popular than kids with more desirable names, and later in life unattractive or unpopular names lead to more rejection by potential romantic partners in online dating sites.[3]

What you name your child can matter.

Intentional naming can also have spiritual benefits. In Hebrew, a name embodies a person's unique character traits and God-given gifts, functioning as a "spiritual call sign."[4] If you, too, choose your child's name intentionally, considering the character traits and prophetic gifts you believe God has for them, then every time you call them by name, you're reinforcing who they are and who they will become.

Again, what you name your child can matter.

Naming traditionally

Tradition in any given culture may influence what and how a person's name is intentionally bestowed. In a myriad of cultures, naming a child is also a great occasion with festivities. Here are a few broad cultural examples that illustrate this point and might prompt you to consider how your own culture or family traditions have influenced what you named or will name your child.

Hebrew Culture

Hebrew names are usually given to a newborn boy on the eighth day after birth during what's called a *brit milah* or *bris* when he's circumcised.[5] Genesis 21:3–4 confirms this tradition:

Abraham gave the name Isaac to the son Sarah bore to him. When his son Isaac was eight days old, Abraham circumcised him, as God had commanded him.

39

Girls are named by their father in the synagogue when he's called up during the reading of the Torah. The naming can take place soon after the birth, up to forty days, or when the new mother can attend the ceremony as well. Sephardic Jews call the naming of a daughter the "presentation of the daughter" in their celebration.[6]

African Culture

Many traditions in African culture include a great celebration when naming a baby, normally within one week of the child's birth. An elder in the family is given the privilege of presenting the name to the newborn by whispering in the ear of the child so the baby is introduced to their name before everyone else.[7] In West African culture, the naming festivities happen around a week after the baby is born but no later than ten days post birth. The Akan people believe the soul decides the name of a child depending on what day it chooses to be born, and they're named after that day of the week. Based on this custom, a child born on Edwoada, which means Monday in the Akan language, would be named Kwadwo if a boy and Adwoa if a girl.[8]

Indian Culture

India also has many cultures and traditions that influence the naming of newborns. Some customs include naming a baby within eight days or up to six weeks. Family is involved from the moment the baby is born. Hindu customs name a baby at twelve days with a naming ceremony called *Namkaran*. The new dad is given the privilege of being the first person to speak the name to the baby.[9]

Chinese Culture

Parents of Chinese descent may continue in the old tradition and prepare to name their child with careful consideration of the character associated with the meaning of the name to be given. For naming girls according to old Chinese customs, they search for names that are unique and describe something beautiful, like Sweet Willow or Morning Star. Words that define characteristics like strength and bravery are given to boys. The baby is given an official name around thirty days after they're born.

Some parents may give each of their children the same word in their name, called a generation name or a variation of the same name, such as Yuan-Chun, Ying-Chun, and Xi-Chun. Each name has the word *Chun* in it. Yuan-Chun means "First Spring," Ying-Chun means "Welcome Spring," and Xi-Chun means "Cherish Spring." I think you get the picture.

Spanish Culture

Most Spanish parents have adopted the practice of naming their children with both the paternal and maternal surnames. The paternal surname is listed first, then the maternal surname. In more recent years, some countries have allowed parents to change the order of the surnames.[10]

Western Culture

A common Western tradition is "namesaking"[11]—naming a child after a beloved family member, a parent, or as the second in line. For instance, we often see both a "senior" and a "junior" in a family, especially when naming a boy, such as William Sr. and William Jr. Of course, the latter will most likely have a nickname as well, even if it's simply "Junior."

Events and circumstances around naming

Names are also known to be given around certain events and circumstances that occur, especially in the Bible.

After giving birth,

Rachel was about to die, but with her last breath she named the baby Ben-oni (which means "son of my sorrow"). The baby's father, however, called him Benjamin (which means "son of my right hand").

Genesis 35:18 NLT

Rachel named her son during the most sorrowful time in her life. The birth of a child normally brings joy, but in this case it did not. Jacob, however, turned a sad occasion into a time of strength by changing his name to Benjamin.

Eli's daughter-in-law named her son as she was giving birth:

She named the child Ichabod (which means "Where is the glory?"), for she said, "Israel's glory is gone." She named him this because the Ark of God had been captured and because her father-in-law and husband were dead.

1 Samuel 4:21 NLT

How awful. I would not want to be a reminder that God had departed a place. But what a challenging time to be born and then be given a name that meant the glory had departed. Having a constant reminder of the tragic time in which you were born, as if you were to blame, would be like a dark cloud following you everywhere. The Bible doesn't give any follow-up information after Ichabod's birth, but I can only imagine that was the beginning of his troubles.

Did any event or circumstance influence what you named your child or might influence how you name a child in the future—hopefully, a good one?

When God chooses your child's name

Scripture reveals how God instructed many parents to give their children a specific name. Mary, the mother of Jesus, was instructed through angelic visitation to name her son Jesus, because His birth introduced the world to God incarnate. Luke 1:31–32 gives this account:

> You will conceive and give birth to a son, and you are to give Him the name Jesus. He will be great and will be called the Son of the Most High. The Lord God will give Him the throne of His father David.

God was intentional. Jesus was to have the name that speaks to His purpose.

John the Baptist's parents, Zechariah and Elizabeth, also gave him his name as God instructed through an angel:

> The angel said to him, "Do not be afraid, Zechariah, because your prayer has been heard. Your wife Elizabeth will bear you a son, and you are to give him the name John. He will be a joy and delight to you, and many will rejoice at his birth, for he will be great in the sight of the Lord. He shall never take wine or strong drink, and he will be filled with the Holy Spirit even from his mother's womb."
>
> Luke 1:13–15

This personal story comes to mind. I had not chosen Joshua for my youngest son's name, but although God didn't send an angel to tell me, I learned he had another name waiting for him.

After this son's birth, I was wheeled off to surgery. One of the two nurses attending to him while I was gone told my husband he looked like his name should be Joshua, and the other one said he looked more like the name she suggested, which became his middle name. His dad agreed and settled on our son's first and middle name before I returned to my room. At first, I protested. But looking back, I wouldn't change a thing.

The name you choose for your child matters. Be open to intentional naming and God's leading in all aspects of the process. Then teach your child the meaning of their name and how and why it was chosen.

Prayer can reverse the negative impact of a name

Of course, if your child has been living for years with a name you and perhaps they as well are concerned about, suddenly switching to a new name is probably not the best option. You can, however, ask God to remove any stigma attached to your child's name as in Jabez's case. Jabez's mother had a difficult time during his delivery, so she named him Jabez, which means "sorrow" or "pain."

This didn't sit well with Jabez, so he cried out to God, "If only You would bless me and enlarge my territory! May Your hand be with me and keep me from harm, so that I will be free from pain" (1 Chronicles 4:10). God heard his simple but powerful prayer asking Him to bless, protect, and expand his life to reverse the negative impact of his name's meaning. The latter part of verse 10 states, "God granted the request of Jabez."

Developing Seeds of Greatness

Our job as parents is to provide all the guidance we can from the time our child is born to when they reach maturation and master self-sufficiency. Doing so helps put them on the path to what is destined for them. And as I said in chapter 1, I believe every child is born with seeds of greatness in them. Although some seeds are never cultivated, the possibilities are unlimited in what they can achieve.

Natural seeds need to be planted in the right soil and at the right time in order to grow. They also need water, nutrients, and sunlight. Seeds of greatness need to be nurtured, too, and here are all four requirements for them to grow:

44

1. the right environment to express, develop, or practice the skill, talent, or gift
2. positive feedback and encouragement
3. assistance from a skilled professional or an organization that focuses on the development of the specific skill, talent, or gift
4. a place to display the skill, talent, or gift

Let's examine the following aspects of fostering growth and achievement in your child: providing guidance, redirecting their behavior when necessary, and reassuring them of your love.

Providing guidance

First, before you try to provide guidance for your child, ask God for His guidance. Parenting is not easy and requires much prayer. You will make mistakes. But remind yourself that you're human, that God is the one who knows your future and theirs, and that you can help them one step at a time. Each child is also different, and raising them will be based on their individual destiny.

Since the idea is to help your child develop their seeds of greatness, let's look at seven definitions for the word *develop*:

1. to make visible or manifest
2. to work out the possibilities of
3. to create or produce especially by deliberate effort over time
4. to make active or promote the growth of
5. to cause to evolve or unfold gradually
6. to lead or conduct (something) through a succession of states or changes each of which is preparatory for the next
7. to expand by a process of growth[12]

45

I've formulated these definitions into successive steps for parents to help their kids develop their seeds of greatness, to mature and reach their destiny.

1. Make the seed visible

For a seed of greatness to become visible, it needs nurturing. It may still be largely hidden and underdeveloped, but with your help it can make its appearance and begin to bud.

Mary, the mother of Jesus, knew He would do great things. That's why she approached Him at the wedding in Cana when there was no more wine. He told her it was not the right time for Him to display His gifts, but she ignored what He said because she saw the opportunity for Him to make His gift visible.

It was certainly the right environment for Him to do so, though. The hosts were desperate, Mary provided the encouragement needed, and the rest is history. Jesus instructed the servers to fill the stone water pots with water and start serving. Everyone knew the servers should be pouring water, so imagine their shock and excitement as they instead poured wine.

Let's take for example a seed of greatness in music. If a child begins to show interest in singing, taps his fingers on the beat, or expresses other musical talent in formative years, then providing music lessons will help unlock and develop that seed. But greatness in music comes not just through lessons but through countless hours of practice and perfecting a skill even if the skill seems to come with ease. This is also a part of making a seed visible.

I have vivid memories of friends who started pecking on the church organ every chance they got until they developed an ear for musical notes and chords, eventually becoming skillful enough to play as musical director. The cringing sounds of an unskillful beginner can become melodious with discipline and determination.

Another friend asked to play drums during our church services, but no one wanted him to because his "playing" was horrible. It had no steady beat. I can picture it as though it were yesterday—his awkwardly adjusting himself on the seat, placing his foot on the foot pedal, and attempting to hit the snare, the cymbals, and then the bass drum. Over time, however, the awkwardness gave way to a steady beat and skill. His hidden talent had evolved. The seed for music had sprouted and grown.

Everyone needs somewhere to practice and hone their skills—although, if necessary, it may be in a basement or on the far end of the house. But the seed must be made visible.

2. Explore the possibilities

Depending on how readily your child's seeds of greatness are revealed, this step might be the first for you rather than the second.

God has an expected end for each of us, and with your help your child can develop the skills and hidden talents He gave them to reach that destiny. *Merriam-Webster's* defines the word *destiny* as "a predetermined course of events."[13] It also means "a predetermined state or end," with the connotation of "something foreordained and often suggests a great or noble course or end."[14]

God has specific thoughts about each of our lives, and once again, a great example is how He predetermined the prophet Jeremiah's destiny before he was born and shared it with him during a time he was unsure of who he was called to be: "Before I formed you in the womb I knew you and before you were born I set you apart and appointed you as a prophet to the nations" (Jeremiah 1:5). Your child's destiny was in the mind of God before they were ever born, and as He formed them physically, intricately woven into the fiber of their being was what they could become.

Isaac sought God to give him and his wife, Rebekah, a child. They soon became pregnant with not one but two babies.

But then Rebekah discerned a struggle between her unborn twins and asked God for insight into what was wrong. God revealed that the babies would each have a large number of descendants—two great nations in the future continually in opposition. He told Rebekah, "One people shall be stronger than the other, and the older shall serve the younger" (Genesis 25:23 NKJV).

Jacob's offspring became the twelve tribes of Israel, a nation chosen by God. Esau, Jacob's brother, and his descendants, the Edomites, warred against Israel until they were ultimately destroyed.

Story time right before daily naps when my sons were little was perfect for engaging them in conversation about who they could become. I talked to them about things they wanted to be when they grew up, but I also shared how important it was to build a relationship with God and know their purpose. My main responsibility as a parent was to steward the precious souls God had entrusted to me. My job was to pour into them the things of God and ignite a fire in them to embrace their purpose.

Take time to talk with your child about their future as they grow. Ask them what their aspirations are. (Be careful, however, not to try to live out your own dreams and aspirations through them.) Once you know what their desires are, you can help them put a plan in motion to achieve what they would like to become. There will be many times when those plans are unclear. Not to worry. Plans will develop as they grow.

We're capable of doing so many things if we put our minds to them, plan, and prepare. Thomas Edison once said, "If we all did the things we are really capable of doing, we would literally astound ourselves." Encourage and allow your kid to try several things they're interested in before settling on anything specific. In time, the seeds of greatness will lead them on the road to their purpose, and destiny will be revealed.

3. Deliberately invest

As with the earlier example about musically inclined children, invest in the development of your child's skills, talents, and gifts. Two definitions for the word *effort* are "conscious exertion of power" and "hard work."[15] These sum up what's required for parents to aid in the success of their kids.

Take interest in what your child is interested in. Observe what they seem to be good at naturally, their strengths and weaknesses, and what they're capable of achieving. As their parent, you know how hard you can push your son or daughter. Then make a commitment to work hard and make sacrifices too.

As I've mentioned before, all four of my sons are musically gifted. They started singing first, and then I pushed them to play instruments. I discerned that if they could sing, they could play an instrument. I'm sure they heard me saying over and over (like a broken record for those of you who still embrace or at least remember vinyl), "You can do anything you put your mind to." I still believe that saying today, and I apply it in my own life when I'm challenged to develop a gift still in seed form. I looked for opportunities that would expand their musical gifts, including piano lessons, joining choir, and countless hours of practice singing and playing instruments.

I guess they believed me at some point, because they did begin to play several instruments. I knew they had an ear for music; they just needed to take the melody from a song and put it in their hands.

Consider the father of celebrated tennis pros Venus and Serena Williams, who identified seeds of greatness for the game in his daughters and then sacrificially invested in their development despite having no skill for tennis himself. Who knows what level of success your child can reach when great investment is made in them?

4. Promote the growth

One synonym for the word *promote* is the word *encourage*. Make your child feel comfortable and safe in the growth process as their seeds of greatness are developed. Encourage them. This is especially important when it comes to any guidance God gives them directly. Until they've learned to hear His voice for themselves, you will be God's voice to them. But they should never be afraid to come to you with anything they've heard from God.

When my granddaughter was around five or six, she had a divine encounter at my house. We were getting ready to go out, and I was in the bathroom putting on makeup. She was in the living room dancing around. Suddenly, she came running to the bathroom door. Excited and scared at the same time, she said, "Gigi, I just saw an angel."

My reaction was shock. I said, "Where did you see it? What was it doing?" I'm always excited for any divine encounter whether or not I'm the one experiencing it.

"It was in the living room by the sofa. It was just there hovering."

"What did it look like?" I asked.

"It was bright and white."

This was a precious moment, so I told her that when God shows up like that, He wants to share something. I told her God speaks to us, and He can speak to her.

Just as I was explaining these things, she shushed me. "Gigi! He's speaking to me now! He's speaking!"

I was so moved that God would speak to her that I cried. I called her parents with great excitement and shared her encounter. The Holy Spirit showed up in an unusual way at my house. I was so glad my granddaughter felt comfortable enough to share her God experience with me. It was beautiful and still warms my heart today.

5. Evolve—gradually

It's okay to get there over time. Accomplishments are more appreciated when each step in the process has been achieved. Hard work and challenges are a given, but be patient and consistent with your child. When the right opportunities come, they'll be ready, because they prepared for such a time as this.

Esther was coached by her uncle Mordecai on how to conduct herself before and after she became queen, and it was that kind of coaching that saved a nation. Her gift was to exhibit wisdom in her position as a monarch. She fasted and prayed to God for a strategy, and God answered. Wisdom in turn produced favor. Had she not prepared, she would have experienced tragedy. Preparation may require years of consistency to get one major opportunity to display the gift that has taken years to develop.

Turning to music again, practice makes perfect. At first, what you hear may just seem like noise. No particular skill or sound. Just clanging and banging. No specific melody or tune. But if you can endure the noise day in and day out, you'll eventually start hearing the hoped-for sound and skill.

When he was younger, one of my sons sang all day every day—in the shower and throughout the house. He was developing his craft, but this routine got on everyone's nerves. We cringed at every note. Up the scale. Down the scale. Over and over. It was familiar, though. A good friend did the same thing growing up. Every morning before school you could hear the belting of soprano coming from an open window. After school the singing continued like an encore, especially if she'd been given the task to learn a new song to lead at church.

The years of practice paid off for both my son and my friend. Now I could listen to them sing all day. And when they had opportunity to share their gifts more publicly, they were ready.

6. Lead the change

Here are some ways you can (and frankly, should) lead your child in the way they should go (see Proverbs 22:6):

- *Follow your own advice and convictions*—Be willing to do what you ask your child to do. Sometimes that means the little things. For example, if you require them to clean their room, keep yours clean too. They will do what they see you do, not just what you say.
- *Be honest and truthful*—Be honest with your kid. Tell the truth. Kids are smarter than you think. If you're not honest, they'll figure that out.
- *Admit to mistakes and wrongdoing*—Admit when you've made a mistake or done something wrong. And apologize. An apology goes a long way. Your child will respect you more when they know you can say you're sorry.
- *Practice forgiveness*—Remember, your child is watching you. If you hold grudges, they will too. Kids mimic the behavior of their parents even when they know it's wrong.
- *Don't be afraid to fail*—Try even if it means possible failure, and don't be afraid to try again. This will teach your child perseverance and tenacity and build confidence.
- *Put in the work for success*—Do what it takes to succeed. If your kids see your work ethic, it will introduce them to the world of setting goals and achieving. And don't forget to celebrate the small victories along the way.
- *Challenge yourself as well*—It's easy to challenge your child, but maybe there's something you always wanted to do but were too scared to do it. Maybe you need to

challenge yourself. After putting them on hold for more than twenty years, I decided to go back to school to finish my bachelor's degree and then get my master's. I wanted to be an example to my sons and show them how important higher education is, just as I'd shown them how important their walk with God is.

I must say it was challenging to work full-time, pastor a church, travel for ministry, raise my kids, and go to school all at the same time, but I didn't give up on my education even though many times I wanted to. I was able to earn both degrees.

7. Expand the process

If your child is talented in multiple areas, you might need to help them focus on one gift at a time, mastering it before they move on. Attempting to become an expert at more than one gift at the same time can be exhausting and paralyzing.

This rule has exceptions, of course. Some kids seem to master whatever they put their minds to and have no problem mastering multiple gifts simultaneously. I was one of those exceptions. I was naturally gifted at sports. I played softball, volleyball, and basketball and ran track all while keeping a high GPA. My parents never pushed me; I pushed myself.

Each child is different, so parent them accordingly. Your child may be a self-starter or you may have to do a little nudging. Either way, if you see the potential, help them expand it.

Redirecting their behavior

Every child's behavior needs to be redirected at times. Even Jesus' parents did so. When they discovered He wasn't with them as they were returning home from a trip, Mary and Joseph were worried that something bad may have happened to Him. As parents, all sorts of thoughts probably bombarded their minds. He could have been injured. Or worse, kidnapped or dead.

> Finally, after three days they found Him in the temple courts, sitting among the teachers, listening to them and asking them questions. And all who heard Him were astounded at His understanding and His answers. When His parents saw Him, they were astonished. "Child, why have You done this to us?" His mother asked. "Your father and I have been anxiously searching for You."
>
> Luke 2:46–48

The dialogue between them was interesting, to say the least. But Jesus was reminded that He was still a child under His parents' care, and He went home with them that day as an obedient son (Luke 2:48–51). The young Jesus learned a valuable lesson and never went off on His own again. From that time on He followed the rules, and it showed: "Jesus grew in wisdom and stature, and in favor with God and man" (Luke 2:52).

Old-school parenting is big on discipline, but redirecting behavior is a creative approach to steering a child into the path of following rules. Don't neglect to do it, though. If you don't, you open the opportunity to spoil your child or make them think they're above discipline. Both have the potential to create other issues, perhaps major ones.

Reassuring them of your love

Our kids need to know we care and that we want what's best for them. We can reassure them by loving them unconditionally and taking the time to tell them we love them.

I grew up in an era when the words *I love you* weren't always expressed from the lips. Yet love was implied because we had a nice place to live, food to eat, and clothes to wear. It was good, however, to hear the words spoken.

When your child is sure you love them, they'll be more apt to trust your guidance.

————

In this chapter, we explored many aspects of how to become your child's destiny helper, aiding you in recognizing and cultivating their seeds of greatness, supporting them when gifts and skills need to be nurtured, providing them with godly guidance, leading them by example, and reassuring them with your love.

Now if you're ready, let me turn your attention to a couple of activities below for how to build a prophetic foundation with your child that will help them reach their full potential and purpose.

PROPHETIC ACTIVITY

After completing the three tasks below, ask God to show you if you need to take any steps in regard to your child's name.

- If you don't already know it, find the meaning of your son or daughter's name.
- Research the culture that name seems to be associated with.
- Determine if the meaning of the name has or could have a positive or negative impact on your child's life.

Building a Prophetic Foundation

Building a prophetic foundation is like laying the foundation of a house. It's the most essential component of what's being constructed. Before walls can be framed and drywalled, the ground must be prepared and staked off. After excavation, the ground is leveled, and concrete is poured. And the taller the building, the deeper the foundation must be to support the weight of the structure.

Positioning for prophetic stability—and indeed, greatness—also requires a deep foundation. In Luke 6:47–48, Jesus says,

> I will show you what he is like who comes to Me and hears My words and acts on them: He is like a man building a house, who dug down deep and laid his foundation on the rock. When the flood came, the torrent crashed against that house but could not shake it, because it was well built.

This doesn't mean this follower of Christ in Jesus' illustration is better than any other person, but with a deep foundation in the Lord, he'll be prepared for any challenge that comes his way. He'll be prepared for the greatness God intends for his life.

Queen Elizabeth II comes to mind when thinking about preparation for greatness. Though a member of the British royal family, she wasn't originally next in line for the throne. But with her uncle's abdication, her father became king, and from that time on she was groomed for her eventual ascension to the throne. Privately educated with a focus on constitutional history, math, and other subjects,[1] she was also prepared to address world affairs, entertain diplomats, and deal with any crisis during her coming reign.

When her father died, the young princess stepped into her destiny. Taking the throne, she became Queen of the United Kingdom, along with other Commonwealth realms, and during her reign of more than seventy years, she became the longest reigning monarch of Great Britain, surpassing her great-great-grandmother Queen Victoria, who reigned for sixty-three years and 216 days.[2]

Could it be that God had preordained her birth and caused the pivot so she would ascend to the throne? It's highly likely. Sometimes He takes the unassuming and causes a repositioning to bring about purpose.

The story of brothers Jacob and Esau is one biblical example of how God pivoted greatness and impact on the earth. Jacob was the second-born twin to his parents, Isaac and Rebekah. Esau, being the firstborn, was destined to receive the birthright and blessing of his father. Esau was groomed by his father to become a great leader and hunter. Jacob, on the other hand, was taught to farm and grow food.

The Hebrew tradition of birthright and blessing was passed down from Abraham to Isaac. Now Isaac was tasked with the responsibility to do the same. The birthright—or *berachot* in Hebrew—is the spiritual leadership and authority as head of the family transferred from the father to the first son, and the blessing—or *beracha* in Hebrew—is the double portion of possessions given to the first son as well.

It's interesting that Esau didn't value his birthright. Perhaps he thought it was a given that, since he was the oldest, he would automatically receive it even though he made a deal with his brother over a bowl of soup. The Bible doesn't say if Isaac and Rebekah discussed whether the birthright was up for grabs or if the brothers' secret deal was revealed. However, one article suggests the issue may have come up:

> According to the Malbim (the great biblical commentator at the time of the Jewish Enlightenment in the 18th century), Rebekah did speak to her husband regarding the twins, and clearly explained why she believed that Jacob—and not Esau—deserved the inheritance.[3]

This was the first major pivot taking place in the lineage of Abraham since his receiving the blessing from God. Abraham was the first of his kind, and he conferred the same blessing on his promised son, Isaac. Isaac in turn was supposed to continue the tradition, but he inadvertently released the blessing over Jacob instead of Esau after being deceived by Jacob and his mother. Esau's timing was off as he came in a little too late. He missed the blessing. Jacob was now the rightful owner of the birthright and the blessing. He received the spiritual authority and double blessing conferred by his father.

This was a great deal. Scripture confirmed that the older would serve the younger when Rebekah was pregnant and God declared it: "Two nations are in your womb, and two peoples from within you will be separated; one people will be stronger than the other, and the older will serve the younger" (Genesis 25:23).

Positioning for greatness doesn't come without challenges. Although this prophecy came to pass, that doesn't mean it was easy. Jacob was secretly sent away to live with his uncle. There would be quite a few years and much hardship before Jacob would take his place as a spiritual leader.

Lay a Deep Foundation

Laying a building's foundation requires multiple steps in the construction process. Who would have thought a prophetic foundation would be layered? But it must secure everything that will stand on it. As for a building, it must be able to bear the weight.

The key word is *construction*, and the word *construct* is defined as "to make or form by combining or arranging parts or elements."[4] As we said earlier, before a building goes up, the foundation has to be dug out, and the depth of the foundation depends on what's being constructed. For someone whose destiny is to make a great impact in their generation, greater care must be taken to ensure that depth of character and integrity are instilled.

Steps in laying a prophetic foundation include the following two:

1. Break ground and excavate—character and virtues

At this stage in the process, everything is dug up, removing anything of little to no impact on spiritual growth. Character and virtues are reinforced, and a leveling of sorts takes place. It's important that your child understands right from wrong, is a free moral agent, and can make their own choices.

Kids must also understand that every decision can have consequences or benefits. For instance, if they tell a lie, that untruth can backfire. When the truth is revealed, you might then view them as untrustworthy. An example of a benefit could be their deciding to not participate in bullying a classmate, thereby avoiding being disciplined when others were.

Scripture encourages children to obey their parents:

Listen, my son, to your father's instruction, and do not forsake the teaching of your mother. For they are a garland of grace on your head and a pendant around your neck.

Proverbs 1:8–9

Children, obey your parents in the Lord, for this is right. "Honor your father and mother" (which is the first commandment with a promise), "that it may go well with you and that you may have a long life on the earth."

Ephesians 6:1–3

This is the time to start teaching your child to please God and why and how to live a life that strives for moral excellence. The book of Proverbs is a great place to begin. In that book of the Bible, King Solomon shares what he learned from his parents from childhood—how he should conduct his behavior, types of people to avoid, and what to strive for.

2. Pour and inspect—input and testing

Once character has been established and actively integrated into a child's lifestyle, character will be tested. Pour, pour, and pour to ensure your son or daughter has a well-rounded start. Similar to pouring footings in construction, this stage is important as it will help bear and distribute the weight of their purpose when it's fully evolved. Samuel grew up around corruption, yet his foundation was one of integrity, hearing and obeying God. It's possible to build a godly foundation in the midst of worldly views.

I have a personal example about how pouring into a life can make all the difference. During a Wednesday night Bible study service, when my kids were really young, they were squirming and annoying one another rather than sitting quietly still. They knew the routine, but their patience had worn thin.

I'd had enough. I decided I was going to get what God had for me even if I had to sit out in the foyer, so out to the foyer we went. I think the kids were inwardly excited, because they could move about without catching the "mom" eye from me. You know, that look a mom gives when a child has done something wrong and they know they're in trouble, but she can't do anything about it because they're in public. Yeah. That one. But I was determined not to be distracted. I wanted to hear the teaching on prayer. I needed to hear that teaching.

The pastor went through the preliminaries and then turned on the tape player. (Yes, we had cassette tapes back then.) I was straining to hear every word through the crack of the double doors. The teaching series began with a male voice with a very distinct tone. I had seen this man on Christian television before. He was Dr. Larry Lea from Tulsa, Oklahoma. He started his series using the Lord's Prayer found in the book of Matthew.

For the first time, those verses came alive in my heart. Oh, I had learned this prayer and recited it often, but never had I heard anyone dissect it, bring life to it, and teach it or illustrate it like that. I heard Dr. Lea's voice say, "Our Father, which art in heaven, hallowed be thy name. The word *hallowed* means to praise and glorify. Now *you* praise Him and magnify His name." His words went out not only to the in-person audience present at the original recording but also to the few dozen parishioners now gathered in our white concrete-block church. We all joined in.

I had found a missing piece in my walk with God. Up to this point, I'd thought I had a decent prayer life, but I must admit I struggled for two and a half years before moving back to Florida. My prayer life had reached a plateau. I was in what I call a wilderness season, a time when it's challenging to hear God's voice and to pray. I wanted to pray, but there were no words. It was like my spirit was hollow. For the first time as a believer, my prayer life was struggling. I had no unction to pray.

But on this night, I found what I was looking for. With my heart delighted and dancing inside me, I could hardly contain my joy. God knew I needed this. For me. For my seed. With every word I hungered more for Him. And later I came to understand that I had been challenged to increase my hunger for God that night.

I came out of that season with victory. I went on to teach my kids everything I learned about prayer through that series and made it digestible and fun for them to learn.

Over the years there would be many more seasons just like that, but many more victories too. And with each new victory came a new anointing.

Pour into your kids to give them the foundation they need, inspecting their progress along the way.

Build the House Well

Now let's consider Samuel, who from birth was prepared to be used by God. Hannah, his mother, had bombarded heaven for his existence and sowed him as a seed to serve God all his life. She prayed for and birthed a prophet needed for Israel at that time. God allowed her void, taunting, and unfulfilled desire for children to pray the will of God into existence. ("Children are a gift from the LORD; they are a reward from him"—Psalm 127:3.)

Due to Hannah's instilling a foundation in Samuel for his purpose, he was prepared to live in the temple. She used the first five years of his life to pour into him and then told him it was time for him to enter the temple. In his sixth year, he was taken to the temple to serve. One can imagine that she and her husband would speak to Eli the priest to arrange for Samuel to intern, train, and begin apprenticeship in the temple.

Hannah visited annually to inquire about her son's well-being and to bring him new garments. She was monitoring his growth physically and spiritually. He was doing well, learning the voice of God and recognizing the state of the priesthood. Eli had assumed she was inebriated as she poured out her soul to God long ago, but surely Samuel would make a difference.

Samuel grew up around the things of God, assisting Eli, who could barely see. As Samuel served, he observed the corrupt sons of Eli, yet he managed to remain unscathed by the corruption. Eli no doubt raised his sons to walk upright before the Lord; however, at some point they began to change. I'll take one guess: It probably started when Eli was no longer able to see as well as before. His sons, tasked with increased responsibilities, took advantage and started abusing their authority in the temple.[5]

What's interesting, though, is that Eli slightly reprimanded them, but not to the point of removing them from the priesthood, because he indirectly benefited from their abuse. But that didn't make it right for them or Eli.

Meanwhile, Samuel was learning to hear God:

> The LORD called Samuel. Samuel answered, "Here I am." And he ran to Eli and said, "Here I am; you called me." But Eli said, "I did not call; go back and lie down." So he went and lay down. Again the LORD called, "Samuel!" And Samuel got up and went to Eli and said, "Here I am; you called me." "My son," Eli said, "I did not call; go back and lie down." Now Samuel did not yet know the LORD: The word of the LORD had not yet been revealed to him. A third time the LORD called, "Samuel!" And Samuel got up and went to Eli and said, "Here I am; you called me." Then Eli realized that the LORD was calling the boy. So Eli told Samuel, "Go and lie down, and if he calls you, say, 'Speak, LORD, for your servant is listening.'"
>
> 1 Samuel 3:4–9

Eli was well acquainted with ministering in the service of the Lord as he had experienced a lengthy priesthood. His life was even more intriguing because he served in dual roles. He was one of the last priests and judges. A descendant after the order of Aaron, the priest appointed by God to serve while assisting Moses. A judge in succession to Samson and the last before the reign of kings in Israel began.[6] Eli's assignment to young Samuel was to teach him the customs of serving in the temple, purification rituals, duties pertaining to handling sacrifices, and being an intercessor between man and God.

Eli discerned that God wanted to speak to Samuel and instructed him on what to do. This was a major lesson for Samuel. He was learning how to recognize God's voice. How did Eli sense it was God calling Samuel? As a servant of God, he had experienced that voice many times.

Let's dissect this memorable moment and perhaps realize we may have had similar experiences.

- Samuel is in the temple in the presence of God.
- Samuel is awakened in the middle of the night hearing a voice calling his name.
- Samuel hears the voice call him three times. It's not revealed whether the voice is audible; however, it is enough to get Samuel's attention.
- The recurrence of the call means that God is persistent and intentional in getting Samuel's attention.
- God wants to speak specifically to Samuel. Eli is in the temple, too, but God wants to get the message to Samuel to share with Eli.
- Eli teaches Samuel how to recognize God's voice.
- God gives a prophetic warning to Eli through Samuel.
- Samuel is afraid to share God's message with Eli.
- Samuel is truthful with Eli and holds nothing back.
- Eli accepts God's message as divine judgment for his disobedience.

Here are some takeaways from what we dissected in the story of Samuel and Eli. Can you think of any additional ones?

- It's important to get into the presence of God.
- Create an atmosphere of prayer and worship.
- Wait for God to speak.
- Be prepared to listen to what He has to say.
- Write down what you hear.

Let's pause to talk about three important ways we can ensure our times of prayer are effective, habits we can teach our children:

1. *Learn to recognize God's voice.* God still speaks today, but the challenge is to recognize His voice when He speaks. We may not realize it, but talking to God in prayer is a two-way conversation. After we've shared our hearts with Him, we shouldn't rush off to other things but wait a few moments in silence, intently listening for His "still small voice." Like Elijah, we can get caught up looking for God to use theatrics to speak to us. But God spoke in a simple way. No great winds, hail, or brimstone. Just simple words.

> Then the LORD said, "Go out and stand on the mountain before the LORD. Behold, the LORD is about to pass by." And a great and mighty wind tore into the mountains and shattered the rocks before the LORD, but the LORD was not in the wind. After the wind there was an earthquake, but the LORD was not in the earthquake. After the earthquake there was a fire, but the LORD was not in the fire. And after the fire came a still, small voice. When Elijah heard it, he wrapped his face in his cloak and went

out and stood at the mouth of the cave. Suddenly
a voice came to him and said, "What are you doing
here, Elijah?"

1 Kings 19:11–13

2. *Keep out the noise.* Elijah encountered the earth quak-
ing and hurricane-force winds, but it was just noise.
The interference we face today is a different kind of
noise. The noise of technology. The noise of busyness.
And this noise interferes with tuning in to the frequency
on which His voice speaks. His voice is drowned out by
everything around us. God used the example in 1 Kings
19 to show Elijah how to cancel out the noise and
search for His voice. We must do the same. At times, we
have to turn it all off—unplug from everything to hear
Him speaking clearly.

3. *Capture what God says.* It's a good idea to keep a
prayer journal nearby to write down what you hear
while in prayer. Most often in prayer, I can be found
with a notebook or using the notes feature in my phone
to capture God's message. Teach your kids to do the
same.

With Samuel, Eli had another chance to learn from his mistakes with his sons, to establish and construct a better foundation than he had with them. Let's be careful to teach our kids
how to avoid the pitfalls we may have experienced.

Implement the Fruit and Gifts of the Spirit

Sarah and Abraham acted in haste to receive the promise God
had given them for a son, and it caused turmoil within the
family. When parents are impatient, disastrous circumstances

occur as in their case. Had Sarah continued to wait, Ishmael would not have been conceived, avoiding two contentious nations. As the foundation is being constructed, we must learn to rely on God and grow spiritually with the fruit and gifts given by the Holy Spirit.

Everything hinges on God's love. The love that moved God to send His Son on a mission to redeem mankind from their lost state is the same love the foundation every human operating in spiritual gifts should be built upon. There are nine gifts of the Spirit listed in Scripture, just as there are nine fruits of the Spirit: "The fruit of the Spirit is love, joy, peace, patience, kindness, goodness, faithfulness, gentleness, and self-control" (Galatians 5:22–23).

Just like natural fruit, the fruit of the Spirit grows when cultivated intentionally, and individuals are responsible for growing their own fruit. The more fruit, the better character is shaped and moral excellence formed. Teach young kids about the fruit of the Spirit and encourage them to exhibit character by practicing the fruit actively. Be sure to share on the level of the child so they understand what the fruits are and how important they are to God.

Unlike the fruit, the gifts of the Spirit are distinctive in how they're exhibited through divine endowments. These gifts cannot be earned, although they can be sharpened. God distributes these gifts to people at His will. There are different gifts, but the same Spirit. There are different ministries, but God uses them all. There are different ways of working, but the same God works all things in all people.

The gifts of the Spirit can be grouped into three categories: power gifts, speaking gifts, and mind gifts. The power gifts are gifts of healing, the gift of faith, and the working of miracles. Healing is the only one listed as plural, meaning healing gifts can manifest in various ways of operation. The speaking gifts include the gift of prophecy, diverse kinds of tongues, and the interpretation of tongues. The mind gifts are the word of knowledge, the word of wisdom, and discerning of spirits.[7]

Power Gifts	Speaking Gifts	Mind Gifts
Gifts of Healing	Gift of Prophecy	Word of Knowledge
Gift of Faith	Different Kinds of Tongues	Word of Wisdom
Working of Miracles	Interpretation of Tongues	Discerning of Spirits

Each gift of the Spirit is complemented by a fruit of the Spirit.[8] For example, the gift of prophecy is connected to the fruit of goodness. For better clarity, here are the categorized gifts of the Spirit shown with their correlating fruit:

Power Gifts	Correlating Fruit
Gifts of Healing	Longsuffering
Gift of Faith	Peace
Working of Miracles	Faith

Speaking Gifts	Correlating Fruit
Gift of Prophecy	Goodness
Different Kinds of Tongues	Gentleness
Interpretation of Tongues	Self-control

Mind Gifts	Correlating Fruit
Word of Knowledge	Joy
Word of Wisdom	Love
Discerning of Spirits	Faithfulness

Gifts start as seeds that need to be cultivated once they become active. Before the gift of healing was activated in my life, it lay dormant for many years.

Gifts of healing

God has used me in the gift of healing for years, but it began as a seed. As a teenager, I would often be drawn to people who were sick, on crutches, or in wheelchairs. When passing them in public, I would have an overwhelming urge to pray for them, but I was afraid.

Many thoughts ran through my mind. What if they weren't healed? I would be embarrassed. What if they got mad because I prayed for them? What if they declined my offer to pray for them? I remember being in church on one occasion and in a vision seeing a man's chest open up while he was walking down the aisle. God spoke to me that He was showing me a sickness in the man's body. Inside his chest was black. It was a spirit of infirmity.

Another time during revival, the guest preacher called for those with spiritual gifts to come forward to the altar for prayer. The preacher specifically asked for those with the gift of healing. I was really afraid, but I stepped out of my seat and got in line. When my turn came for prayer and activation of the gift, the word of the Lord went forth that God would use me in the gift of healing as precisely as a surgeon's hands in the operating room.

Working of miracles

Modern-day miracles do occur. I grew up in a religious organization where the gifts of the Spirit flowed freely and personal testimonies about miracles were often shared.

One single mother didn't have enough food for everyone in her family. But she prayed, cooked the little food she had, and the food was miraculously sufficient. Similar to Jesus' feeding the multitude, it was multiplied to meet a need.

Another woman was driving when the brakes on her vehicle went out as she was approaching a stop sign. She had little time to respond, but she remembered a recent Bible study teaching and exercised her faith by commanding the car to stop. It did, and she shouted in sheer amazement! Everyone was on the edge of their seats as she shared this story in Sunday service.

But she still needed to get to her destination, with more stop signs to encounter. "Every time I needed the car to stop," she said, "I loudly commanded it, saying, 'Stop car!' and the car obeyed."

I know these events may seem preposterous to some, but the supernatural is active in the lives of those who believe.

———

In this chapter, I hope you've learned how to assist your child in building a prophetic foundation that's solid in the things of God and valuable lessons on spiritual fruit and the gifts of the Spirit and how each correlates with the other.

If your younger child is the right age for a word matching game, consider implementing what you've learned for teaching them about spiritual fruit and the gifts of the Spirit through this prophetic activity.

PROPHETIC ACTIVITY

Play this matching game with your child to teach them that every fruit of the Spirit has an accompanying gift. If your child doesn't read, see the last bullet point.

- First, write each fruit and gift of the Spirit on a plain sheet of paper or colored construction paper and cut them out individually.
- Then give your child a short lesson on what you learned about the fruit of the Spirit and the gifts of the Spirit in this chapter.
- Last, spread out the pieces and then have your child match each fruit with the corresponding gift.
- If your child doesn't read, cut out eighteen pieces of colored construction paper with two pieces of the same color to match each correlating fruit and gift of the

Spirit. For example, red construction paper can be used for the corresponding fruit of the Spirit "love" and the gift of the Spirit "word of wisdom." Don't forget to label each. Then work with your child to match the colors of each and explain to them why the colors are the same.

Activating Your Child's Prophetic Gift

Prophetic gifts can be grouped into four main categories: (1) hearing from God, (2) seeing what God is showing you, (3) speaking what you see or hear from God, and (4) moving or operating in the gifts of the Spirit. Prophetic gifts are powered by the Holy Spirit for His purpose and can show up and be activated in the life of a person at His will.

And because every prophetic gift must be proven, once activated, they're tested as they're developing. For example, Samuel's gift was proven just as the gifts of other prophets in the Bible were. From the time he was a boy, God confirmed His words through Samuel:

> As Samuel grew up, the LORD was with him, and everything Samuel said proved to be reliable. And all Israel, from Dan in the north to Beersheba in the south, knew that Samuel was confirmed as a prophet of the LORD. The LORD continued to appear at Shiloh and gave messages to Samuel there at the Tabernacle.
>
> 1 Samuel 3:19–21 NLT

When I ministered in a town in Georgia some years ago, I met a young lady with an amazing voice. The pastors there told me that before she was filled with the Holy Spirit, she couldn't sing a note. It may sound farfetched, but the young lady and her mother confirmed this was true.

That story is an example of how some gifts are clearly defined in the Scriptures and some are not. For example, although gifts of healing are referenced in the Bible, it indicates that the healing gift can be performed in multiple ways. Here are just a few:

Through the laying on of hands:

At sunset, all who were ill with various diseases were brought to Jesus, and laying His hands on each one, He healed them.

Luke 4:40

Through sending a word of healing to someone without being in their presence:

The centurion answered, "Lord, I am not worthy to have You come under my roof. But just say the word, and my servant will be healed." . . . Then Jesus said to the centurion, "Go! As you have believed, so will it be done for you." And his servant was healed at that very hour.

Matthew 8:8, 13

Through using prayer cloths or aprons as a point of contact:

Even handkerchiefs or face-towels or aprons that had touched his skin were brought to the sick, and their diseases left them and the evil spirits came out [of them].

Acts 19:12 AMP

Through using the shadow of someone as they pass by a crowded audience:

> As a result, people brought the sick into the streets and laid them on beds and mats, so that at least Peter's shadow might fall on some of them as he passed by. Crowds also gathered from the towns around Jerusalem, bringing their sick and those tormented by impure spirits, and all of them were healed.
>
> Acts 5:15–16

Dreams

Dreams play out a story or event as if the person dreaming is watching a movie. Sometimes the person is in the dream but only as the recorder or the one behind the lens capturing what's being shown. That dreams (or "night visions") aren't specifically listed as one of the nine gifts of the Spirit doesn't mean they're not prophetic gifts from God. God uses various types of dreams as tools to communicate with us. This is why dreams fall under the realm of prophetic gifts.

When I teach about dreams, I encourage people to write down their dreams in detail, noting the environment or setting, colors, shapes, the emotions they experienced, and what occurred as meticulously as possible. Even the smallest detail could be significant. The goal is to document everything they can from the dream to help accurately interpret it.

Dreams may be "what you see is what you get" kinds of dreams. They may have a literal meaning. Someone who has them sees the future—what will happen—and the dream is self-explanatory. Other dreams are shrouded with symbolism. The person dreaming sees symbols, and the dream needs to be dissected and analyzed to bring understanding. In other words, it needs to be interpreted.

To dissect dreams, I like to record details from them in what's called a "fishbone diagram." You can find samples on the internet, and I recommend doing this for visions as well. (We'll talk about visions soon.) Some dreams deal with time and timetables denoting specific time periods or the length of time before the events of a dream will come to pass. I've had multiple dreams where I saw a clock about to strike twelve and so knew what I'd dreamed would come to pass very soon.

Interpreting dreams

The ability to interpret symbolic dreams comes from God. According to Daniel 2:22, *He* is the revealer of hidden things and secrets waiting to unfold:

> God speaks time and again, but a person may not notice it. In a dream, a vision in the night, when deep sleep falls on people as they slumber on their beds, He uncovers their ears at that time.
>
> HCSB

Let's talk about a couple of men of the Bible to whom God gave the gift of interpreting dreams.

Joseph

Joseph, a vivid dreamer, told his family about his dreams even though he didn't understand them. And telling those dreams often got him in trouble with his family. As a matter of fact, his being a dreamer was one of the reasons his brothers hated him and sold him into slavery.

Joseph was naive and shared his dreams out of innocence, but he didn't know how to interpret them, and it would be a long time before he did. His gift to interpret dreams had not yet been activated. With any gift comes great responsibility, and I believe Joseph needed to mature before the gift of interpretation could be activated. That maturity came during his years of slavery in Egypt.

After the king's chief cupbearer and baker had dreams, they said to Joseph:

> "There is no one to interpret them." Then Joseph said to them, "Don't interpretations belong to God? Tell me your dreams."
>
> Genesis 40:8 HCSB

Later, the cupbearer said to Pharaoh:

> A young Hebrew, a slave of the captain of the guards, was with us there. We told him our dreams, he interpreted our dreams for us, and each had its own interpretation. It turned out just the way he interpreted them to us: I was restored to my position, and the other man was hanged.
>
> Genesis 41:12–13 HCSB

Quite a few years had passed from when Joseph was a young lad who dreamed to when he was a man who had matured through hardship, now sharing the meaning of dreams with his fellow prisoners. His gift to interpret dreams was proven, and just as Scripture explains, his words were true. Then his gift opened the door to an opportunity to interpret a dream for the pharaoh:

> Pharaoh said to Joseph, "I have had a dream, and no one can interpret it. But I have heard it said about you that you can hear a dream and interpret it." "I am not able to," Joseph answered Pharaoh. "It is God who will give Pharaoh a favorable answer."
>
> Genesis 41:15–16 HCSB

Giving God the credit, Joseph prayed for the interpretation of the dream, and God revealed it. Notice I said he prayed for the interpretation. It's important to ask God to reveal a dream's meaning or activate the gift to interpret it. It's easy to come up with our own ideas of what a dream may mean, but in order to know exactly what God is saying, we need to ask Him.

I believe this was in God's plan—to cause Joseph to gain his freedom and swing into reality the series of dreams he'd had so many years earlier. It's amazing how God will weave the lives of various people through a process of events to bring His plan to pass. He planned to use Joseph and his dreams to save a nation.

Daniel

Daniel is another person in Scripture who had the gift to interpret dreams. And when King Nebuchadnezzar asked him if he could interpret his dreams, he not only interpreted one for him, but like Joseph, he gave the credit to God before doing so: "No wise man, enchanter, magician or diviner can explain to the king the mystery he has asked about, but there is a God in heaven who reveals mysteries" (Daniel 2:27–28 NIV).

Daniel and his friends had survived a scary ordeal involving lions and a furnace of fire, but that didn't deter him from serving God and putting Him first. Daniel's gift shined the light on and brought glory to God. After he interpreted King Nebuchadnezzar's troubling dream, "The king said to Daniel, 'Your God is indeed God of gods, Lord of kings, and a revealer of mysteries, since you were able to reveal this mystery'" (Daniel 2:47 HCSB).

Daniel and his friends Shadrach, Meshach, and Abednego were committed to living a life pleasing to God and had refused to take part in worshiping the king. They would rather have died than bow to an idol. And because they lived according to godly principles, Scripture notes that "God gave these four young men knowledge and understanding in every kind of literature and wisdom" (Daniel 1:17 HCSB). It also says,

In every matter of wisdom and understanding that the king consulted them about, he found them 10 times better than all the diviner-priests and mediums in his entire kingdom.

verse 20 HCSB

Now let's discuss three types of dreams: symbolic, warning, and literal.

Symbolic dreams

Some dreams have symbolism in them, meaning what you see may not be reality but a representation. Unlike literal dreams, symbolic dreams need to be dissected or interpreted to receive the intended message. A person may see an array of images, numbers, people, animals, places, or things, and the same dream may occur more than once or in a series of dreams related to the same message.

Let's explore the Scriptures deeper to expand meanings pertaining to common symbols and numbers.

In the Greek, the number seven can, among other things, mean completion, and the number ten can, among other things, represent governmental authority. Numbers in dreams may also identify chronological time—days, months, or years. Let's look at the dreams Pharaoh's cupbearer and baker had and how Joseph interpreted the numbers in them:

> The chief cupbearer told his dream to Joseph: "In my dream there was a vine in front of me. On the vine were three branches. As soon as it budded, its blossoms came out and its clusters ripened into grapes. . . .
>
> "This is its interpretation," Joseph said to him. "The three branches are three days. . . ."
>
> When the chief baker saw that the interpretation was positive, he said to Joseph, "I also had a dream. Three baskets of white bread were on my head. . . ."

"This is its interpretation," Joseph replied. "The three baskets are three days."

Genesis 40:9–10, 12, 16, 18 HCSB

Each servant saw the number three—three branches and three baskets. Although the items counted were different, branches and baskets, they each were interpreted by Joseph as three days. The number three itself was a confirmation of what was inevitable. The days were represented differently in each dream, once by branches and again by baskets, showing that various items can have the same meaning depending on the dream and who is dreaming it.

The chief cupbearer saw the branches budding with blossoms that became clusters of grapes. This portion of his dream revealed favor and longevity in his position. But the baskets the baker saw on his head revealed that he was a burden. Both led to deliberation by Pharaoh. For one man the result was favorable, and for the other it was not.

Joseph also interpreted Pharaoh's two-part dream of an uncertain future and impending famine:

Pharaoh said to Joseph: "In my dream I was standing on the bank of the Nile, when seven well-fed, healthy-looking cows came up from the Nile and began to graze among the reeds. After them, seven other cows—ugly, very sickly, and thin—came up. I've never seen such ugly ones as these in all the land of Egypt. Then the thin, ugly cows ate the first seven well-fed cows."

Genesis 41:17–20 HCSB

Then he added:

In my dream I had also seen seven heads of grain, plump and ripe, coming up on one stalk. After them, seven heads of grain—withered, thin, and scorched by the east wind—sprouted up. The thin heads of grain swallowed the seven plump ones.

Genesis 41:22–24 HCSB

Joseph interpreted the number seven as years—in this case, seven abundant years followed by seven years of harsh famine. Pharaoh's dream was a warning of imminent famine in the future.

We'll discuss warning dreams next, but for now, let's practice dissecting and recording the first part of Pharaoh's dream—again, a process I recommend for dreamers to aid in the interpretation of their dreams:

- the symbols—the numbers seven and two sets of animals, one set well-fed and the other set emaciated
- the scene—a description of the animals' physical appearance and what each set was doing
- the setting—Egypt near the river Nile

Here are examples using the numbers four, six, and fifty along with the Hebrew and Greek words for them and their prophetic meanings to assist with interpretation when dreaming about numbers.[1] I've included the Hebrew and Greek meanings since the Bible was mostly translated from these two languages and they provide more detail into the meaning of each one. Prophetic meanings have also been included to give more insight for each number.

Four (4)
Hebrew word: *arba*
Greek word: *tesera* or *tetra*
Hebrew and prophetic meaning: The number four is associated with the fourth letter of the Hebrew alphabet, *dalet*,

and the symbol is a door. A few meanings include an opportunity, entryway, pathway, and "God has helped us."

Six (6)
Hebrew word: *shesh*
Greek word: *hex*
Hebrew and prophetic meaning: The number six is associated with the Hebrew letter *vav*, and the symbol is a nail. Meanings include to add to something, a hook, to fasten, and to secure something. The number six is also associated with the number of man, as in the book of Revelation.

Fifty (50)
Hebrew word: *chamishshim*
Greek word: *pentékonta*
Hebrew and prophetic meaning: The number fifty is associated with the letter *nun* in the Hebrew alphabet, and the symbol is a swimming fish. The meaning includes being alive and active. This number is also associated with Pentecost, when the Holy Spirit sat upon those waiting in the upper room, and it is celebrated by Christians during a Hebrew holiday known as the Feast of Weeks or the Feast of Shavuot that takes place fifty days after Resurrection Day or Easter.[2]

Warning dreams

When God wants to send a warning about what's coming, He may allow someone to have a dream about it. One dictionary defines a warning as "an indication providing evidence of impending danger, difficulty, or misfortune."[3]

As mentioned earlier, one example of a warning dream is the dream God gave Jesus' earthly father, Joseph, telling him that Jesus was in danger and to move to Egypt immediately:

An angel of the Lord appeared to Joseph in a dream: "Get up!" he said. "Take the Child and His mother and flee to Egypt.

Stay there until I tell you, for Herod is going to search for the Child to kill Him."

Matthew 2:13

Had Joseph not taken God's warning of impending danger seriously, King Herod would have found Jesus and killed Him, altering His destiny and cutting short His assignment on earth. Likewise, God will give dreams of warning to parents to remove their children from immediate threats that could alter their purpose and might be destructive if not heeded. It's imperative to pay attention to the dreams we have about our kids.

Literal dreams

Do you or your child dream about things before they happen? That's called a literal dream. You see the event or situation in advance. The scriptural example of the angel appearing to Joseph is also a literal dream. The dream revealed that King Herod would search for the infant Jesus to kill Him, but Joseph, being a step ahead, avoids the tragedy. Matthew 2:16 confirms this:

When Herod saw that he had been outwitted by the Magi, he was filled with rage. Sending orders, he put to death all the boys in Bethlehem and its vicinity who were two years old and under, according to the time he had learned from the Magi.

Decades ago, one Friday night I had a dream about a friend marrying. I saw the wedding dress and the ring. When I woke up on Saturday morning, the dream was still fresh in my mind, but to my knowledge she was not married or planning to be. But I couldn't shake the dream and felt it was from God. I even shared it with others. A short time later I discovered that my friend had married, in secret, the very weekend I had the dream.

From this experience, I learned that if God speaks to us through a dream, we must hold on to the message even if no one believes us.

Visions

Just like dreams, visions allow access into the spirit realm, at times revealing glimpses into the future or providing some supernatural insight. But the person is not in the sleep realm. They're awake.

Many people in Scripture encountered visions. Here's one that comes to mind:

> Peter went up on the roof to pray. He became hungry and wanted something to eat, and while the meal was being prepared, he fell into a trance. He saw heaven opened and something like a large sheet being let down to earth by its four corners. It contained all kinds of four-footed animals, as well as reptiles and birds. Then a voice told him, "Get up, Peter. Kill and eat."
>
> Acts 10:9–13 NIV

God used this vision to reveal two changes concerning Hebrew customs: (1) nothing God blesses is unclean, so it's allowed to be eaten, and (2) the gospel Jesus had preached to Jews was now spreading to non-Jewish people—or Gentiles.

As a young minister in my midtwenties, one Sunday morning I experienced an open-eye vision. I was sitting with other clergy on the platform when suddenly the supernatural realm opened and a holographic video appeared. It was a scene of the three Hebrew boys and Jesus in the fiery furnace. I could still see the audience peering through, but I could also see these four figures moving about unbothered by any heat or flames.

I reasoned within myself: *I'm not sure what's going on here. This isn't normal. I can still see the people in this church. But how?* After what seemed like an eternity, the vision disappeared, and I was back to seeing only the people sitting in the pews. I had not been asleep or even sleepy. I'd been wide awake, having this supernatural encounter while the service took place.

I can't tell you why I had the vision, but I do know God reveals His secrets as He wills. The apostle Paul had a divine encounter that confused him. Had he had an out-of-body experience or not? Second Corinthians 12:2 describes his encounter: "I know a man in Christ who fourteen years ago was caught up to the third heaven. Whether it was in the body or out of it I do not know, but God knows."

Jeremiah was a prophet of visions. It seems as if God often asked him what he'd seen and used his gift to show him future plans for His people, Israel. Here's an example:

> The word of the LORD came to me, asking, "Jeremiah, what do you see?" "I see a branch of an almond tree," I replied. "You have observed correctly," said the LORD, "for I am watching over My word to accomplish it."
>
> Jeremiah 1:11–12

Many of the visions Jeremiah saw were filled with symbolism, and he accurately conveyed what he saw to God. Then God revealed the meaning of the symbolism. Sometimes it was a vision of warning. Sometimes it was a vision to reveal the hearts of His people.

Prophecy

A gift is an endowment that cannot be earned, and one definition of prophecy is "the gift of communicating and enforcing revealed truth."[4] The word *prophecy* is derived from two Greek roots: *pro*, meaning "before," and *phemi*, which means to "make clear" or forthtell by a God-given endowment.[5] To predict the future, if you will, by the mind and will of God, what He desires, and how often. Prophecy is directed by the Holy Spirit, not our human spirit.

The forthtelling of little glimpses of the future was common in my house and church. My family was used to the gifts of the Spirit flowing, and my children were encouraged in the development of their gifts during prayer, worship service, or Bible study. When the atmosphere is right, it's easy to flow in prophetic gifts.

Prophets of old would call for a minstrel or someone who could play music to assist in stirring up the gifts. Worship music can activate prophetic gifts and even drive out demonic spirits. While in the pasture tending to his father's sheep, David played his instrument and wrote many prophetic songs that foretold of the future Christ and His earthly assignment. On multiple occasions, his music also drove out demons plaguing King Saul.

Let's look at what we mean by the spirit of prophecy, the company of prophets, and the prophet's office.

The spirit of prophecy

Anyone who sits under the spirit of prophecy can prophesy under that umbrella even if they don't have the gift of prophecy. Saul, the future king of Israel, had such an experience when he met the prophet Samuel and the prophetic team that followed him. Those who witnessed it were confused and wanted to know if Saul was now a prophet:

> When Saul and his servant arrived at Gibeah, a group of prophets met him. Then the Spirit of God rushed upon him, and he prophesied along with them. All those who had formerly known Saul and saw him prophesying with the prophets asked one another, "What has happened to the son of Kish? Is Saul also among the prophets?"
>
> 1 Samuel 10:10–11

A company of prophets

Let's discuss two major prophets in the Old Testament who exhibited the concept *company of prophets.*

Elijah facilitated a school of the prophets to which he traveled at times, as did Samuel. The sons of those prophets were the ones who followed Elijah and Elisha as they journeyed before Elijah was taken up into heaven by a chariot of fire. Also known as a company of prophets, they traveled as a group to every place Elijah and Elisha went and told Elisha that his master would be caught up on the same day it happened.

In King Saul's pursuit of David, he was told that David was living in Ramah with Samuel, and as soon as he heard that, he ordered soldiers to go and arrest him: "When they saw the group of prophets prophesying, with Samuel leading them, the Spirit of God came upon them, and Saul's messengers also began to prophesy" (1 Samuel 19:20). This is a good example of a company of prophets in action and shows again how anyone can come under the umbrella of the spirit of prophecy when in the company of prophets actively operating in prophetic gifts. In the New International Version of the Bible, the term *company of the prophets* is used several times in 1 and 2 Kings.

My sons were immersed in the prophetic as they grew up around prophetic schools conducted by me and friends of mine and participated in prophetic ministry when they were very young. They witnessed firsthand companies of prophets ministering, and although youths, their prophetic gifts were activated while among the prophets. They would sometimes assist in the services, holding a recording device when personal prophecy occurred to capture the words of the Lord on behalf of the person receiving the prophetic words.

The prophet's office

The office of the prophet is occupied by one who has been proven and qualified to hold the title of prophet. It is to be taken seriously. Modern-day church is divided when it comes to prophets. Part of the body of Christ believes prophets died out and there are no prophets of today, and the other part does believe the office of the prophet is still relevant.

What happens when prophets miss it? I mean proven prophets. Did they really hear from God? Did they make up something and share it as God's word? Did they prophesy presumptuously? Did their personal feelings affect what they said? These are all the same questions addressed during biblical times concerning prophets who prophesied for money and prestige or under pressure from a certain group to give a favorable word.

These areas should be addressed early so that the gifted one understands that the gift flows through flawed individuals and must be continuously purified. Purification is important. How do prophets keep themselves and their gifts purified? I'm glad you asked.

- Refrain from ungodly conversations such as gossip and vulgarity.
- Read God's Word. The Scriptures act as a cleansing agent and will wash away impure thoughts.
- Get in the presence of God often. Take time to worship and pray. Anywhere. Everywhere. Every day. All day. Talks with God are essential.

When prophets are pure, their gifts can flow with purity without hidden agendas or opinions. Knowing how to share a prophetic word as God's mouthpiece is also important. Prophets can get into trouble when taking it upon themselves to interpret what they think God is saying. They need to learn to remove their personal feelings and opinions from what God says.

Jonah had this problem when he allowed his personal feelings to interfere with his assignment. God told him to go to Nineveh to compel the people in the city to repent, but he didn't think they deserved God's mercy. So he boarded a ship and went in the opposite direction of where God was sending him.

This decision cost Jonah an intense Sheol experience, a kind of death, in a large fish's belly. Then after a horrible three days, he was finally freed. During the experience, Jonah had plenty of time to think about God's mercy, and after the fish spit him out, he had no problem going wherever God wanted to send him. As a matter of fact, he ran straight to Nineveh and shared God's word, and it brought great repentance to the city.

When releasing God's word, prophets must learn to

- put aside personal emotions
- leave out their own opinions
- say only what God said

Sometimes God speaks a word to the prophet that's up for interpretation. For example, if He says to tell someone He's going to give them a child, it may mean they will give life to a child naturally. Or it may mean they will adopt a child. But what did God specifically say? Only *I am going to give them a child*. A prophet must release God's word just the way He said it.

In this chapter, we covered quite a bit about activating your child's prophetic gifts; provided the distinctions between prophecy, the spirit of prophecy, the gift of prophecy, companies of prophets, and the office of the prophet; and brought understanding to various types of dreams and visions and their purpose. With what you've learned, you can use worship, the Word, and prayer as tools to assist your child in activating their prophetic gifts.

PROPHETIC ACTIVITY

Help your child create a dream journal, and then make your time using it together special. They'll look forward to it.

- Use a tablet, spiral-bound notebook, or a binder with loose-leaf paper.
- When your child has a dream, have them write down what they saw in detail and draw pictures as well. If your child is too young to write, write down the dream and its details for them, and then ask them to draw what they saw. Don't forget to date the dream so you can look back and see what's happened in the weeks or months following.

Acknowledging Your Child's Spiritual Experiences

Let's first establish that the spirit realm is real and supernatural things beyond human comprehension can and do occur. Have you ever experienced something brushing past you when no one was physically there? Have you ever seen or experienced something that defies nature? Or perhaps you've taken a photo and uninvited subjects showed up in it, and you knew they weren't there when you snapped it. Have you ever heard sounds in the night and knew they defied any earthly sound you'd ever heard?

Both good and evil spirits exist in the spirit world, and from time to time they enter the earthly realm. Inhabitants of the spirit world are mentioned throughout the Scriptures from Genesis to Revelation, such as angels (cherubim, seraphim, messengers, warriors), and, yes, demons and Satan himself.

The spirit world generally can't be seen by those in the earthly realm, which exhibits what is physical. But a few spiritually intuitive individuals are the exception—though at times they may not understand what they're seeing in the realm they're peering into. And when children experience them, it's important for them to be believed—for their experiences to be acknowledged, especially by their parents.

The apostle Paul recounted a supernatural experience when he was unable to adequately depict what he saw with mere words or provide an accurate description of which realm he was in. The summation of his encounter included being exposed to the spirit realm, seeing and hearing things that aren't normally seen or heard in the physical realm:

> This boasting will do no good, but I must go on. I will reluctantly tell about visions and revelations from the Lord. I was caught up to the third heaven fourteen years ago. Whether I was in my body or out of my body, I don't know—only God knows. Yes, only God knows whether I was in my body or outside my body. But I do know that I was caught up to paradise and heard things so astounding that they cannot be expressed in words, things no human is allowed to tell.
>
> 2 Corinthians 12:1–4 NLT

The wonder of a child is filled with curiosity, and that curiosity can lead to interactive encounters in the spirit world. Kids may not immediately perceive whether a supernatural experience is good or bad. They may have ungodly encounters with spirits that at first appear friendly to gain their trust. But the spirits' intent is to influence and, if possible, ultimately gain possession to carry out their mission.

Once the child's trust is gained, unusual supernatural experiences may occur, such as the spirits speaking with the child, doors opening and closing by themselves, or items falling off shelves. Seeing things no one else sees can be traumatic, and young kids with prophetic gifts may be taunted with such things.

Pay attention to what your child says when they're trying to tell you what they experience. Just because you can't see what they're seeing doesn't mean what they're seeing isn't real. This will also build trust with them so they'll tell you more of what they're seeing in the future. If you don't believe them, it can cause them to suffer in silence—at least until they learn how to properly deal with these experiences. That's another reason it's imperative that you listen to them and believe what they tell you. You need to teach them.

At age twelve, one of my former parishioners had traumatic dreams about things like planes crashing and other tragic events. She thought she was crazy. But I explained that she wasn't crazy, that God was showing her these things so she could pray about them, and that she was a prophetic intercessor. She's now twenty-five years old, says my encouragement helped her understand her gift, and embraces what God shows her and prays accordingly.

Nightmares and Trances

God uses sleep to rejuvenate the body, and He also uses it to send messages to us when we're too busy to receive them when we're awake. But like God, the enemy uses nighttime and the sleep realm. He agitates those he wants to disturb, especially those with prophetic gifts as they are usually more sensitive to the supernatural.

Nightmares can be defined as frightening dreams that occur during REM sleep. The Mayo Clinic further describes a nightmare as "a disturbing dream associated with negative feelings, such as anxiety or fear that awakens you."[1] Their scientific approach identifies several characteristics of a nightmare, which I have adapted and elaborated on here:

- The dream seems real and is quite disturbing, even plaguing the dreamer after waking.

- The dream includes violence, threats of violence, violations, tragedies, or other catastrophic events that disturb the dreamer.
- The dream is emotional, making the dreamer feel fear, sadness, disgust, anger, or anxiousness.
- The dream stays with the dreamer for long periods of time and remains vivid as time passes.
- The dream continues as if scenes from a movie after the dreamer awakes and falls back to sleep.
- The dream leaves a startling effect upon the dreamer.

My youngest son dreaded nighttime because in his dreams he saw things that were real but didn't exist physically. He saw angels, but he also saw demons. He was constantly tormented by demonic spirits until he learned to take authority over them and command them to leave. In the apostle Paul's words about love, its lack of fear, and how perfect love casts out fear, he tells us what fear brings us: "torment" (1 John 4:18 NKJV).

Let's briefly consider trances as well—mentioned, for example, in Acts 10:10 and 22:17. And in 2 Corinthians 12:1–4, Paul told of a trance he experienced. Trances can occur when someone is awake but also when they're asleep. Discussing what they call sleep paralysis, WebMD says this is when the body isn't "moving smoothly through the stages of sleep" and is "a feeling of being conscious but unable to move."[2] Some trances bring a night terror or torment.

If your child has any of these experiences, teach them to pray and take authority over them. You can, of course, also pray this prayer for yourself if you experience nightmares or disturbing trances:

I exercise my God-given authority as a believer in Christ Jesus. I take authority over every demonic spirit that interrupts my sleep. It will not bring torment and terror to me. I will sleep peacefully and without fear. In Jesus' name, amen.

Kids must be taught how fear operates and how to take authority over it. Once fear has been dispelled, the torment stops, and if a nightmare does occasionally occur, it's a good idea to search the root of what may have allowed fear back in.

Paranormal Demonic Activity

When the eyes of a child—or an adult, for that matter—are open to the supernatural, they can see and experience otherworldly things. Those otherworldly things can be viewed in the form of images or interactive spirit beings that move and speak. Diabolical in nature, demon spirits use fear as the root to continue antagonizing their subject. Once fear has taken root, the door is open for more torment.

I can relate to the experience of demonic activity. Around age seven or eight, while sleeping one night between my younger brother and sister in our old full-sized, iron-framed bed, I was awakened when a witch walked into our room. She stood at the foot of our bed. I couldn't see her face, but I could make out her silhouette. Evil was in the room. She never said a word, but as I peeped over my covers in horror, she took her pointy finger and touched my foot. I was so scared that I immediately put the covers over my head and prayed, hoping nothing more would take place. At some point I must have fallen asleep, but I've never forgotten that experience.

It's not normal to be continually disturbed by demonic activity. So if this is occurring with your child, then you should first investigate to see if a door has been opened to allow demonic activity in the home. The enemy looks for ways to torment. He will seek out legal entryways, but he will try to enter illegally too.

I recall a family being plagued by demonic forces many years ago. The grandfather was a practicing warlock. The daughter and grandchildren had distanced themselves, but there was still a door open in the spirit realm and legal access given, so the enemy used that door and access to wreak havoc among them.

As parents, we must guard our kids against attacks both naturally and spiritually. Search your bloodline to make sure there are no open doors the enemy can use to cause torment for you or your child.

Here are some events or doors that allow the enemy legal access for demonic activity:

- The enemy, as we mentioned earlier, will often use bloodline curses and traumatic events—such as a tragedy, a violation, violence, or abuse. According to Matthew 13:25, he will sow weed seeds when men are unaware and then go away for a season only to later return to see if the seeds he's planted have sprung up and begun to choke out the good that was planted.
- The enemy will often use media—horror movies, TV shows, video games, and virtual reality.
- The enemy will often use participation in and use of astrology, horoscopes, palm/psychic readings, tarot card readings, and séances.

Guard What Your Kids See and Hear

Media has played a great role in releasing the spirit of fear into homes ever since the late 1800s when the first horror movie was released, and special effects have evolved to be more realistic than ever. Movies and TV shows project what the mind can imagine or perhaps what has been experienced. Many are based on true occurrences—with some added Hollywood effects, of course. Today it seems the gorier, the more horrific, or the more tragic the better to bring in the most revenue at the box office. These types of films increase the fear factor.

It's up to us as parents to guard the spirits and souls of our kids by guarding what we allow them to see and hear. Disturbing scenes from a movie, TV show, or video game can show up in their dreams, even if they have a fascination for them.

An old children's Sunday school song says little eyes and ears must be careful about what they see and hear. This is also true for adults but ever the more for the kids God has put in our charge to guide and nurture. We have to be mindful of the TV programs, movies, and music that we, too, watch and listen to. We are not of the world, but we are in the world, so we are constantly at war with what's around us. Daily, we can listen to and follow three voices: "God's voice, the enemy's voice, and our voice."[3] When we don't stay attuned with God's voice, we can and will be led astray by the lusts of our own flesh and the voice of the enemy.

We must instill in our children how to stay in the presence of God and hear His voice, and we do this by teaching them Scriptures and how to pray, all the while making sure what they see and hear glorifies Him. You can't keep them from the evils in this world, but you can equip them with how to discern and to cover and protect themselves and their families and friends.

Proverbs 4:23 says, "Above all else, guard your heart, for everything you do flows from it" (NIV). In Scripture, the word *heart* refers to "a person's inner moral and spiritual life . . . the core, the inner essence of who we are."[4]

> A good man brings good things out of the good stored up in his heart, and an evil man brings evil things out of the evil stored up in his heart. For the mouth speaks what the heart is full of.
>
> Luke 6:45 NIV

The LORD said to Samuel, "Don't judge by his appearance or height, for I have rejected him. The LORD doesn't see things the way you see them. People judge by outward appearance, but the LORD looks at the heart."

1 Samuel 16:7 NLT

We must teach our kids the importance of guarding not only their hearts but what they allow in them. For example, Scripture indicates Lucifer was involved with music in heaven before his fall (Ezekiel 28:13 NKJV), and anything and everything he can do to pervert its sound and purity, he will. What we allow to come into our ear gates affects our spirit. And Matthew 6:22 says, "The lamp of the body is the eye. If therefore your eye is good, your whole body will be full of light" (NKJV). The eyes are the window to the soul as described in this verse, and what enters through those gateways will impact the emotions of your child, good or bad.

Author Jessica Van Roekel tackles what to allow your kids to watch and listen to in an article that asks three questions:

1. Does it help or hinder their faith?
2. What behaviors result afterward?
3. What are the prevailing internal thoughts after the entertainment?[5]

In addressing question one, parents, we're responsible for blocking anything that has the potential to disrupt our child's spiritual growth or cause them to derail from their faith.

The second question deals with the impact of what they've seen or heard. Does the result cause negative behavior? Are they showing signs of aggressiveness? If that's the case, they should not have watched that movie or TV show or played that video game.

The response to the last question answers thoughts your child may have after watching what they're allowed to watch. If your son or daughter is depressed or has suicidal thoughts, they should not be allowed to continue watching that type of entertainment.

Using Our Authority in Christ

Before we move on to divine encounters, let's talk about teaching your child how to use their authority in Christ.

As indicated before, it's important that you and your child know who you are in Christ and your spiritual authority over demonic spirits. Luke 10:19 states that the believer has power and authority over the enemy. God has given the believer authority over demonic spirits no matter the age; they only need to be trained on how to use it. Young kids can be trained to use the name of Jesus during an ungodly encounter, and older kids can be trained more extensively to command the demonic spirit to leave.

What is the definition of authority? Authority is "the power to give orders or make decisions: the power or right to direct or control someone or something."[6] But every believer needs training to know how to use the spiritual authority God gives.

What does the training look like? Your child must know that God is their heavenly Father and that they have been delegated as an ambassador from heaven to use His Word to make decisions and give orders that are in alignment with what He said in the Bible. You train them first by teaching them God's Word, then teach them how to apply His Word in their lives. And if anything opposes His Word, then you teach them to combat that opposition by speaking declarations and decrees.

Kenneth Copeland thoroughly discusses our authority in Christ in an article from which we can glean the following spiritual rights, authority, and position God gives believers young and old:

- authority over sin
- authority over Satan and the kingdom of darkness
- a heavenly seat of authority with Christ
- authority to use God's Word when exercising spiritual rights[7]

Teach your child who's learning to exercise their spiritual authority to pray,

> I exercise my God-given authority as a believer in Christ Jesus. I take authority over every demonic spirit in this house. I revoke your legal access to me and my family. I command you to leave now. In Jesus' name, amen.

Divine Encounters

If you've determined that no door has been voluntarily opened to welcome demonic activity, then monitor your child for other experiences, such as angelic visitations.

I've had many divine encounters when I've committed to setting time aside to pray and bask in the presence of God. Once, I canceled all appointments just to be in the presence of God. He met me there in my bedroom in a tremendous way that day and showed me many spiritual things as I prayed and saw angels and heard their assignments to men on the earth. On another occasion, I was in prayer, but I was so tired that I fell asleep. An angel appeared and fed me. It was so real that when I awakened from my sleep, I was rejuvenated to the point that I knew it had been supernatural.

Many divine encounters are recorded in the Bible. We've already mentioned how God visited the young prophet Samuel.

Samuel heard the Lord's audible voice calling him three times, but he didn't realize it was God's. And we've already mentioned Peter sitting on the rooftop waiting to be called to breakfast when God spoke to him. Then there's when the women ran to Jesus' tomb after His crucifixion and an angel appeared and told them that He had risen and was not there. And when Peter was in prison and an angel appeared in his cell:

> An angel of the Lord stood by him, and a light shone in the prison: and he struck Peter on the side and raised him up, saying, "Arise quickly!" And his chains fell off his hands. Then the angel said to him, "Gird yourself and tie on your sandals," and so he did. And he said to him, "Put on your garment and follow me."
>
> Acts 12:7–8 NKJV

As I said earlier, when children tell us their dreams and nightmares, how we respond helps determine if they will trust us enough to tell their stories to us in the future. It also helps them know how to handle spiritual things in the future.

I know someone who's seen angels since she was a child. But she never really told anyone about it until she was in a church service with her friend and heard the Holy Spirit tell her that angels were there in the sanctuary. The Spirit wanted her to point out where they were to her friend.

She argued with the Holy Spirit, because she just knew her friend would think she was crazy. But God was testing her faith and obedience to Him—and He wanted to help her friend as well. She obeyed, and her friend's eyes were opened as well. She was able to see them too.

When this woman shared this experience with me, she was shocked that I didn't brush her off or make her feel as if she was crazy. Instead, I reassured her that she had a rare gift in the spirit realm and that was normal. This made it a lot easier for her to speak about angels and demons with me and others without feeling judged.

———

In this chapter, we discussed supernatural experiences—good experiences in the form of divine visitations and evil ones exhibited through nightmares and demonic activity. We covered how to discern the difference and teaching your kids how to exercise their God-given authority over demon spirits and demonic encounters.

The next chapter is on the power of mentorship, and it's going to be good!

PROPHETIC ACTIVITY

Have you been helping your child capture their dreams as outlined in the prophetic activity at the end of the last chapter? It's not too late to start. Just read the instructions once more and begin.

1. Add any new dreams to the journal, again making sure you date each one. In the process, your child will learn to discern the difference between godly and demonic dreams as well as when a dream is the result of their watching a movie or TV show or playing a video game.

2. Once you've updated the dream journal, complete this spiritual activity assessment on not just your child's behalf but yours. This will help you determine if you need to change some of your entertainment habits as well.

SPIRITUAL ACTIVITY ASSESSMENT

Activity	Description	You	Child(ren)	Notes
Godly Encounter				
Nightmare				
Trance/Sleep Paralysis				
Godly Encounter				
Nightmare				
Trance/Sleep Paralysis				

Understanding the Power of Mentorship

Those with spiritual gifts need a mentor, someone with greater giftings or at least the same gifting and experience to help guide and develop them. Why is it important for children to have mentors? An old African proverb says, "It takes a village to raise a child," and Proverbs 22:6 says, "Train up a child in the way he should go, and when he is old he will not depart from it." Both encompass the importance of mentorship in a child's life.

Mentorship is vital to life and the destiny of every prophetic child, especially as they approach adolescence. Mentoring can help young people deal with challenging life transitions, assist in forming their spiritual identity, and even support them as they safely navigate critical stages in their purpose and destiny.

So what is mentorship? It's a mutual relationship between a mentor and mentee to provide the mentee with support and advice on a personal level to encourage growth and development and overall improvement in their life.

But what is spiritual mentorship? Spiritual mentorship is when someone, usually in ministry and with similar prophetic or other spiritual gifts, takes an inexperienced gifted child or adult under their wing for the purpose of assisting in their spiritual growth and development. There's nothing like a healthy, close, bonded, and supportive relationship between a mentor and mentee that lasts for a significant amount of time and proves to be central to a young person's success.

As I was not raised in a Christian home, I was blessed to receive spiritual mentoring when I committed my life to Christ as a young person. I now realize that throughout the various stages through to adulthood, God gave me many mentorship moments through people who planted seeds to help me grow spiritually and into the woman I am today. The mentoring moments with my female mentors took on various forms ranging from informal gatherings after church to corporate prayer meetings and church services.

The NAOMI Model

What did I learn from these valuable mentoring moments? I came to appreciate those times and understand that successful mentoring relationships all seem to possess similar qualities. And the five traits I've deemed significant for the cultivation of a safe and healthy mentoring connection are what I've termed the NAOMI mentorship model based on Naomi and Ruth's relationship in the Bible:

"Do not urge me to leave you or to turn from following you. For wherever you go, I will go, and wherever you live, I will live; your people will be my people, and your God will be my God. Where you die, I will die, and there I will be buried. May the LORD punish me, and ever so severely, if anything but death separates you and me." When Naomi saw that Ruth was determined to go with her, she stopped trying to persuade her.

Ruth 1:16–18

106

After they both experienced tragic losses and unimaginable grief, Naomi turned her energy from bitterness into mentoring Ruth, who became more than her daughter-in-law. As Naomi poured her energy into Ruth, it softened her bitterness and brought more joy into her life.

Let's explore more of this mentorship model by discussing the details of the acronym NAOMI: Nurturing, Adaptable, Open, Motivational, and Insightful.

Nurturing: The ability to care for and encourage the growth or development of someone is a vital characteristic to building a strong mentorship. Ruth obviously observed Naomi as she provided a nurturing environment in her home. This must have made a lasting impression on Ruth to make her not want to leave Naomi and be willing to follow her and adopt her culture.

Adaptable: Adaptability is required on both parts in every mentoring relationship. Naomi, being the mentor, had to allow Ruth to follow her back to her homeland. And Ruth, already having adapted to Hebrew culture, was willing to abandon all she'd previously known to experience the fullness of Naomi's lifestyle in the land of Judah.

Open: Open communication is essential for the success of any mentorship relationship. Each party needs to feel comfortable and unrestricted to engage in coaching throughout the time allotted. Fostering the relationship in a safe environment helps mentees better navigate life as they learn to wisely apply knowledge and advice given from the mentor.

Motivational: It is the mentor's responsibility to influence and motivate the mentee to want to be better, do better, and grow exponentially. This type of coaching may not be easy, but it is worth it to see the results. Naomi motivated Ruth to enter Boaz's barley field to work. Ruth followed her mentor's instructions, and God's favor ensued, eventually bringing a proposal, marriage, and a place in the lineage of David and Jesus.

Insightful: Wisdom and discernment are imperative when mentoring. The insight of a mentor can shift a mentee's life. As Ruth's mentor, Naomi had insight that Ruth needed a husband. To preserve her family's legacy, she remembered Boaz from her husband's side—a wealthy man. She instructed her to glean in his field and lie at his feet to symbolize her interest in him, and Ruth did as Naomi advised. It was Naomi's insightfulness that brought Ruth and Boaz together, in turn protecting the legacy for generations to come.

Dolly Parton once said, "If your actions create a legacy that inspires others to dream more, learn more, do more and become more, then, you are an excellent leader."[1] All the mentor relationships shared in this chapter have two elements that factor into mentorship in common—the need for trust and a safe environment.

Trust

The mentor-mentee relationship must be built on trust. The mentor must trust God to receive insight and relevant information for the one being mentored. I call it the pouring effect. God pours into the mentor, and the mentor in turn pours into the mentee what has been poured into them. In my thirty-five years of ministry and mentoring, I've learned to ask God to share His desires for and strategies for how to positively affect the lives I've connected with. And even though the mentee learns from the mentor, the mentor learns from the one being mentored.

One of the first things I learned is that trust must be reciprocated. It's not one-sided. In the early years of mentoring, I assumed I would share God-inspired insight and then expect the person I was mentoring to just be open to everything I shared and automatically trust me. That was not the case.

I needed to learn that trust is like communication. It requires both parties to participate. I needed to open myself to being vulnerable if I expected anyone to trust me in the mentor-mentee relationship. I could be vulnerable and still maintain my position as mentor. People look for those who are relatable. Relatability is crucial. Judgment is not needed and should be avoided.

When selecting a mentor for your child, however, be careful that the mentor is someone trustworthy whose character has been proven. Also take note whether your child feels comfortable with the mentor. If they feel uneasy, don't force them to continue the mentorship.

A safe environment

A safe environment for mentorships requires parameters to protect both parties. Meetings should never take place in questionable or unsafe places or for excessive amounts of time. Parents, ensure that mentoring is safe for your child. They trust you and your judgment as their first mentor and expect this to be a positive experience. If you suspect anything other than a positive experience or if your child tells you something detrimental happened, stop immediately and take the appropriate action.

Mentors in the Bible

Now let's look at some mentors in the Bible to see how they helped develop those they mentored and what we can learn from them in our effort to raise our prophetic kids.

We'll study Elijah, Elisha, Jesus, David, Paul, and Naomi. Elijah mentored Elisha, a servant God chose to replace him after he was taken off the scene. Jesus mentored many, including the twelve and the seventy. David mentored four hundred men who went from poverty and brokenness to become great warriors. Paul mentored various people in the early churches, especially Timothy. After taking Elijah's place, Elisha mentored Gehazi, who made wrong choices and paid dearly for them, and Naomi mentored Ruth, who became an ancestor in the bloodline of Christ.

Elijah's mentorship with Elisha

Elijah was a prophet who lived during the reigns of Omri, Ahab, Ahaziah, and Jehoram over Israel. His mission was to speak out against the generational wickedness coming from the palace that was turning its citizens from God. He was fierce and bold and combated the false prophets of Baal in a showdown at Mount Carmel. God used Elijah in the gifts of healings, faith, and miracles. He prayed and shut up the heavens, and for three years it didn't rain, causing a great drought.

As a seasoned prophet, Elijah founded the school of prophets from Bethel to Jericho and provided training to the sons of the prophets and their fathers before them. The sons of the prophets were descendants of those originally trained by Elijah who were skilled in the gift of prophecy. They prophesied to Elisha that Elijah, his master, would be taken away. The accuracy of their prophetic words was phenomenal.

The Bible records only one instance where Elijah cast his mantle on someone. That someone was Elisha, who was working in his father's field when Elijah found him. Elijah carried out the instructions of God and presented Elisha with a unique opportunity to mentor him and prepare him to answer the call of God on his life and continue in all that Elijah had established.

Elijah operated in healings and miracles and performed eight notable miracles. Elisha agreed with God's decision for his life and became Elijah's prodigy. He followed Elijah everywhere God sent him, observing Elijah perform miracles, causing him to desire to do what his mentor did. Elijah tested Elisha's loyalty on several occasions, asking him to stay while he went to Gilgal, Bethel, Jericho, and Jordan. But Elisha knew he needed to follow through to complete his assignment to receive the final impartation:

When they came to the other side, Elijah said to Elisha, "Tell me what I can do for you before I am taken away." And Elisha replied, "Please let me inherit a double share of your spirit and become your successor."

2 Kings 2:9 NLT

Let's not forget that Elijah was a proven prophet whose words came to pass when he prophesied that the false prophetess Jezebel, her husband, King Ahab, and their sons would be destroyed. He also prophesied that King Ahaziah would succumb to his injuries because he didn't ask God if he would recover. Instead, he inquired of the Ekrons' god, Baal-Zebub.

Elijah was perplexed by Elisha's request, but he said if Elisha saw him when he went up, his request would be granted. Elisha had no idea what his mentor meant, but he would soon find out.

As the chariot was taking Elijah up to heaven, something fell to the ground, and Elisha saw it. It was the prophet's mantle. No doubt Elisha never imagined his key to a double portion of what Elijah carried was tied to his cloak, but the garment was not needed in heaven; it was useful only on earth. In wonder and grief, Elisha picked up the only remnant of his master. But did it work only for Elijah? After all, it did belong to him. He wore it everywhere. Could that be what Elijah meant?

Elisha's miracles doubled the number of Elijah's, many occurring in similar fashion to the miracles performed by Elijah.

Elijah trained Elisha in these four ways: (1) to hear the voice of God and speak His heart even when it was controversial, (2) to adhere to the standards of God, (3) to operate in the gifts of the Spirit when prompted by God, and (4) to continue the prophetic training established with the school of the prophets.

What we can learn: We can receive an impartation from a mentor and accomplish double because of that impartation. Elisha was successful in what he asked for from his mentor, and although he didn't immediately understand what he'd received, he came to know the power of that impartation as time progressed.

Elisha's mentorship with Gehazi

Elisha picked up the prophetic mantle and anointing that had been on Elijah and became an established prophet. He chose a servant, Gehazi, to continue the pattern. Gehazi traveled with him and observed the miracles performed just like Elisha did when traveling with Elijah. There was one problem, though. Gehazi failed the greed test. He deceptively caught up with the captain Naaman, who had just been healed in the river Jordan of leprosy and asked for the money and clothes Elisha had just turned down as payment for his healing. Failing this test cost Gehazi his health, his position as Elisha's protégé, and the prophetic mantle and anointing that would have been passed down to him. The same leprosy Naaman was cured of was pronounced on Gehazi.

Elisha conducted the same types of training he himself went through and passed with flying colors. Little did he know that contempt was brewing in the heart of his trainee.

What we can learn: To those with prophetic gifts, it's of great importance to pass the greed test. This is the test presented to Jesus when Satan took Him up on a high pinnacle to tempt Him with worldly treasures. Of course, He passed because He remained focused on what He was called to do and kept His heart pure (Matthew 4:1–10).

Judas Iscariot failed the greed test miserably when he accepted a bribe from the religious council that wanted to destroy Jesus, betraying the Lord. And earlier, when a woman poured expensive perfume on Jesus' feet, he objected, saying, "Why wasn't this perfume sold and the money given to the poor? It was worth a year's wages." This passage from John goes on to tell us, "He did not say this because he cared about the poor but because he was a thief; as keeper of the money bag, he used to help himself to what was put into it" (John 12:5–6 NIV).

Jesus' mentorship with the disciples and others

Jesus chose a dozen men to mentor with various gifts and talents—most with fishing businesses, one who worked for the government collecting taxes, and others whose occupations are not given in Scripture. They all had one thing in common, though: Jesus chose them. He spoke to them individually, saying "Follow me," and they each followed Him into a new world, eyes beholding things bewildering and simultaneously amazing.

The Gospels describe how and when Jesus chose the Twelve. He chose Andrew first, a disciple of His cousin, John the Baptist, perhaps for his passion. Andrew soon told his older brother Simon about his strange and exciting encounter. This is what the brothers were looking for. Something different. Something divine. John the forerunner had introduced them to the one whose shoes he was unworthy to lace. He indeed was the One.

Next came James and his brother, John, who were fishermen too. They were working on their nets when Jesus chose them that fateful day. Then came Philip and Nathanael (also called Bartholomew), and Levi Matthew, the tax collector Jesus found in his tax booth. He said to him, "Follow me." After that, Jesus called Thomas, James (the son of Alphaeus), Thaddeus, Simon the Zealot, and Judas Iscariot.

Jesus developed a relationship with each of them, learned their personalities, and gave nicknames to some. For example, he called Simon by the name Peter, a rock for his tenaciousness, and he nicknamed brothers James and John the sons of thunder because of their heated passion.

After mentoring the Twelve, Jesus sent them out on missions, each with a ministry partner. His strategy is certainly a good one to follow. The Twelve were handpicked to mentor. He knew they were rough around the edges, but He saw their potential. He asked each of them to follow Him and then left the decision up to them. Upon following Him, they observed His teaching and how He interacted with people—many with different spiritual views. When He knew they were ready, His next step was for them to implement what they'd been taught.

Others impacted by Jesus' mentorship besides the Twelve were Cleopas, mentioned in Luke 24:18; Joanna, the wife of Herod's steward, and Susanna, both described in Luke 8:3; Salome and Mary the mother of James, found in Mark 16:1; and Jesus' own family. Jesus' mother, Mary, and His brothers James, Joses, Simon, and Judas (not the Judas who betrayed Him) are listed in Matthew 13:55 (NKJV). They all followed Him as well as all those unnamed, like the more than seventy He trained and sent out (Luke 10:1).

What we can learn: Mentors will observe your personality and character traits, challenge you to apply what you've learned, and discuss whether you've applied those things. Jesus identified gifts and flaws alike in the men He chose to follow Him. Seeing their potential, He was willing to give them a chance to change—even Judas Iscariot, knowing he would one day betray Him. It's okay to be flawed as long as you're honest about who you are and willing to change for the better.

David's mentorship with the four hundred men

It may seem that David became a leader by accident, but it was in God's plan all along. David showed compassion and fortitude for his father's sheep while tending to them in the pasture and defending them when needed. David's passion and boldness were his strongest attributes, and they paved the way for a lifetime opportunity to win a major victory for Israel under King Saul's leadership when its own military was too weak to defeat a chronic enemy. This victory catapulted David into a new arena, where he led the same army that was once paralyzed with fear, too afraid to fight the Philistines, to winning wars.

But this was soon cut short by the same king who appointed David to lead.

As David's victories increased, the victory songs shifted from King Saul being the focus to David being the focus. Saul had killed thousands, but David had killed tens of thousands, and the king was not having it. Filled with jealousy, he labeled David a traitor and put a bounty on his head. There again, this was in God's plan. David had learned many things under Saul's leadership. He learned how to conduct himself in the presence of diplomats as he was invited to live in the palace. He learned how to lead an army and conduct military strategies and exercises. This would help him in the long run.

David found himself a fugitive and hated by his beloved king, so he hid out in the cave of Adullam. But it wasn't long before his family and other men, desperate like him, found out and came to his hideout. Emotionally, David was in no shape to lead anyone, but the men didn't give up and made him their leader.

David began training the men, four hundred of them, to fight skillfully and with grit until they became a fierce paramilitary unit. His mentorship was so impactful that those he trained went from being in distress to conquering everything in their path. Second Samuel 23 tells of the conditions of the men when they came to the cave to make David their mentor.

With David's mentoring, the confidence of the men went through the roof, and as a result, they're listed in the Scriptures as mighty men and known for their courage and strength.

What we can learn: Some mentors tell you to be strong and courageous, but others lead by example and show you how to conquer your fears and build potency. David was that type of leader. He fought alongside those he led and mentored them, showing them how to be victorious even when under attack. David maintained integrity and respect for the leader he had once served. He exhibited grace under fire for sure.

Paul's mentorship with Timothy and the early church

Paul poured into a young believer named Timothy, watching him develop in his faith and grow in the ministry. Paul reminded Timothy to remember his legacy of faith from his mother and grandmother (2 Timothy 1:5). He also encouraged him at times to war with the prophetic words that had been spoken over his life. Timothy became a young pastor under Paul's leadership.

Paul also poured into the New Testament churches and wasn't afraid to provide constructive advice when he saw or heard about things getting out of hand or actions that contradicted God's standards. During those days, there were no phone lines or video communications, so he sent letters to address any issues that arose when he could not be present.

What we can learn: A good mentor will invest in you, remind you of what God has promised you, encourage you to fight for those things promised until what God said comes to pass, and provide advice to you when it's needed.

Naomi's mentorship with Ruth

Naomi and Ruth had a unique relationship as mother-in-law and daughter-in-law, but I think it was more like mother and daughter. When both their husbands died, Ruth had the opportunity to return to her relatives. But she was so impacted by Naomi that she forsook her people and homeland to follow her. Ruth's decision to follow Naomi and forsake her gods to follow Yahweh positioned her to meet Boaz and become an ancestor in the lineage of Jesus: She said to Naomi, "Your people will be my people, and your God will be my God."

What we can learn: The takeaway is that it doesn't matter how you start. With the right mentor you can be positioned to house greatness as we see in Ruth's case. She went from being a widow to marrying a wealthy man and being blessed among women.

Many underestimate the power of mentorship. It's like an unseen umbilical cord attached to ensure the development of a child in the womb, and it can become a lifeline to a child being mentored. A nurturing mentor helps discern lifegiving essentials to the journey while filtering out any waste and toxicity encountered.

You were your child's first mentor, but don't be afraid to involve other mentors who are skillful in gifts similar to your child's to help nurture and develop those gifts.

How the World Mentors Our Kids Too

I once watched a TV show that assigned mentors to young kids who exhibited psychic abilities. The mentors were trained in their abilities as children themselves, and they were teaching these children how to recognize and embrace their gifts. They each took a child to an area known for paranormal activity and then asked them what they saw, heard, and felt.

Sadly, it seems it's more widely accepted for the world to train their own than for the church to teach about prophetic gifts. We have to break what's been considered taboo in the church and start preparing the next generation. Today's society is filled with interest in the supernatural. We should not shun it. The Bible speaks of gifts of the Spirit and how the Holy Spirit moved. The early church operated in it, and so should we. Our kids are drawn into the world because their curiosity into the spirit realm is satisfied through video games, virtual reality, movies, and TV. The church should be on the cutting edge for the supernatural.

We used to be. I grew up in a Spirit-filled church where the supernatural power of God was at work. Every believer young and old was encouraged to experience God. We witnessed young kids filled with the Holy Spirit. Healings taking place was a common occurrence. Cancer was gone. Tumors disappeared.

Creative miracles took place. Legs grew out. It was a phenomenal environment to grow up in spiritually. That is what the kingdom of God looks like.

Mentoring Your Adult Child

Maybe you didn't have the opportunity to impart the things of God into your child when they were young or had the guidance you needed to do so. But if they're an adult—especially if they're actively seeking your advice and support—you can have the chance now. Just remember that they're not a kid anymore. Sometimes your conversations will look messy, but the result can be fruitful.

Consider these points when mentoring your adult child:

- Don't force the opportunity for conversation; this may cause them to become closed-minded. Be patient. Wait until a moment opens up to share, perhaps sparked by a conversation on a particular subject.
- Let them lead the conversation and ask questions.
- Be willing to have meaningful conversation even if their perspective or opinion is different from yours. Really listen to what they have to say. Be respectful.
- Don't make comparisons with others or yourself. That may cause your child to be agitated or hide behind an emotional shell.
- Don't be judgmental or condescending. Treat them as you want to be treated.
- Don't remind them of past failures. They know what their failures are.

In this chapter, we discussed elements of mentoring and biblical examples of mentor-mentee relationships, studying both successes and failures. Before moving on to the next chapter, complete the prophetic activity below. Then we'll learn how to create a balance between daily life and spiritual gifts that will reflect an extension of prophetic service for a lifetime.

PROPHETIC ACTIVITY

Choosing the right mentor can enhance a life, and choosing the wrong mentor can be detrimental to one. Take time to examine how mentors have affected your own life, good or bad, and then what mentorship your child may need.

- Pull out a notebook, tablet, or electronic device and list any mentors you've had.
- Categorize them by life phases or areas of interest, such as career, education, or something personal.
- Consider those mentors' effects on you and your destiny.
- Now record areas where your child may need mentorship and think of a possible mentor for them in each of those areas.

7

Teaching Balance for Lifelong Prophetic Service

It's important to ensure your prophetic child understands the balance between the spiritual and the natural. Their relationship with God is their first priority, but as parents, it's our job to also make sure uniquely childhood experiences aren't neglected. They need to play just as other kids do. This balance is essential and promotes healthy growth all around. But the spiritually gifted often struggle to strike a balance between living a normal life and using their gifts. They can be overwhelmed.

An online search to define the word *balance* revealed these two definitions: (1) "an even distribution of weight enabling someone or something to remain upright and steady,"[1] and (2) a state in which "different elements are equal or in the correct proportions."[2] Let's see how these play out in the life of your child—but in yours as well. A balanced life for a child is reflective of a balanced life for their parent. The struggle is real with everything around us moving all at once. We, too, must find balance in the chaos.

Several components working in harmony help bring balance to the life of those gifted and given to serving God. Learning to balance personal abilities with the wisdom of God and to function in prophetic gifts in alignment with God's heart and desires for your life and still be human is quite the balancing act. At times the gifted are expected to be superhuman and not feel the pressures associated with being gifted. But it's impossible for them to go through life without experiencing the weight of what they've been called to do—to live out that call among family and peers with no reminders of some flaw that appears to nullify their qualification to do what they do and be who they are.

Balance for Parents

Begin with managing priorities at home, work, church, and any other place of responsibility. I once took the FranklinCovey course titled "The 7 Habits of Highly Effective People" to discover ways to increase my effectiveness at home and work. This is what I learned:

No matter the course, if you don't apply what you learned, you'll be back at square one before you receive the certificate of completion. Habit 2 in the seven-habits course (Begin with the End in Mind) and Habit 3 (Put First Things First) were most beneficial for me.[3] They each supported the idea of clear measures when planning to meet goals and prioritizing. Habit 3 is based on four quadrants of time management covering what's necessary, what's effective, what's a distraction, and what's a waste.[4]

Prioritizing in my house when my kids were young was like priming the pump on an old water well—it worked until we had to prime everyone again. It was a big thing for me to have everyone choose and, if necessary, iron what they planned to wear the next day to save time the next morning. And let's not forget date nights requiring babysitters and track meets, basketball games, cheerleading, band practice, and other extracurricular activities children may participate in.

The juggling never stopped. But even just designating one spot to store everyone's backpack or preparing lunches in the evening so everyone can just grab them on the way out the door the next morning can make the difference in getting to school and work on time.

Take time for yourself as you're prioritizing. Even the airline industry recognizes that self-care is a top priority. Passengers are told to put on their own oxygen masks in an emergency before assisting others—even kids—in putting on theirs. Scheduling "me" time will keep you rejuvenated. Self-care is a must when parents are running a household, working full-time jobs, and raising children who have their own lives and schedules.

Don't feel guilty if you take a day or at least a few hours for yourself. Go to a spa or play a round of golf. After you do, you'll be ready to jump back in to support your kids and merge your schedules with theirs.

Balance for Kids

A balanced life is beneficial to your child's mental well-being, but that balance doesn't just happen for them any more than it just happens for you. Let's explore some ways you can help your child achieve the balance they need.

Scheduling

A key component toward balance is scheduling. Your child should be involved in deciding their schedule, but of course, the initial question should be how you can help them balance their life.

Is your child overscheduled? Does anything need to be shifted or even eliminated? Start by asking your child what they think is most important on their schedule. Certain things are mandatory, of course—like spending time with God in prayer, daily Bible reading, and school. But explore how other activities can be scheduled around the mandatories or should even be eliminated if their schedule is overloaded.

Also, sometimes what starts out being of interest to your child becomes mundane or boring to them. Check to see if their attitude has changed about their involvement in the sport, band, choir, and such.

Allow and remind your kid to enjoy life at every stage. Times of fun and recreation should be scheduled just as times of prayer and Bible study are scheduled. And it's okay if they want to sleep in from time to time. They may just need more rest.

Creating overall balance

Education writer Linda Stade wrote an article to help parents create balance in their kids' lives. Here are the five foundational components she believes are required for anyone to achieve balance in life, young or old:

1. Understand yourself.
2. Accept that not everything is under your control.
3. Be aware of your priorities.
4. Choose to live in the moment.
5. Control expectations.[5]

I've adapted these into the following five teaching steps for parents seeking to help their prophetic kids learn how to achieve balance rather than struggle and be overwhelmed.

1. Teach your kid how to understand themselves and who they are. As children go through the growth cycles, they may know who they are in one stage but not in another stage. Support them at every stage and help them

discover their identity as they evolve. One way to help them forge identity is to allow them to discover their individuality at a young age.

2. Teach your kid that some things are outside their control. It may be a challenge for kids to know when things are overwhelming. They may experience frustration without knowing why. Help your child understand what is within their authority to control and what is not.

3. Teach your kid to recognize and then focus on priorities. This can be a tough one, because learning how to prioritize is tricky. Knowing what's essential and what's urgent can be confusing. Teach your child that, for example, if a project is due for a class at school tomorrow, it takes precedence over the one that's not due until next week.

4. Teach your kid to enjoy every stage of life. Children must learn to celebrate and reward themselves at every milestone at any age. Help your child smell the flowers along the way and not wait until they become adults to enjoy life.

5. Teach your kid to manage their expectations. This is another tough one. It's easy to fill our lives with more than we can manage, and then when things don't turn out the way we expected, disappointment and discouragement set in. Teach your child that it's okay to reassess what they're managing and then eliminate what they can no longer manage well—without feeling bad about it.

Living out balance

Teach your child that balance in the prophetic life also looks like this:

- *Accepting accountability for words and actions even if it means suffering consequences.* What happens if your child gives a prophetic word, and it doesn't come to pass? Many prophets and prophetic people release words they thought they heard God say, but then what they revealed doesn't happen. Do we immediately call that person a pseudo-prophet? No. We observe the character of the person and their heart. Being in prophetic ministry since the 1980s, one thing I've learned is that even authentic prophets can miss it. We're human, and at times we allow our humanness to interfere with hearing God. Teach your prophetic child to admit when they've missed it. They can ask God to show them where and how this happened, learn from the mistake, and move on.

• *Living a life of truth and honesty even if it means running the risk of being embarrassed or ridiculed.* We can teach children to stay true to themselves and to God. Integrity is more valuable than gold. Encourage your son or daughter not to worry about how others may respond.

• *Being committed to God's Word and living life accordingly even if that commitment separates us from others.* We want to live our lives pleasing God. Our covenant is with Him, not people. This commitment may cause some friends to walk away from your child because they think they're too radical, but wouldn't your son or daughter rather lose a friendship than lose their relationship with their heavenly Father? I would. Assure them He will send new friends whose values are aligned with theirs.

• *Learning to behave properly and controlling emotions when needed, while being able to express ourselves and not compromising who we are.* Teach your children to never allow themselves to become unhinged

126

emotionally to the point that they get out of character. They can get their point across in a civil manner. The older your child, the easier it will be for them to grasp this concept and live it out.

• *Being empathetic toward others and putting ourselves in their shoes to try to understand their perspective.* Teach your son or daughter to be open to other points of view. To exercise compassion and understanding. They'll be thankful you did as compassion is paid forward when they're in need of it.

Testing

Life can bring about tests that reveal and challenge character flaws that may need correction. Life for kids who are gifted both spiritually and naturally is no different, and they'll encounter one or more of the following tests, need parental advice to cope with what they experience, and learn how to move past potential pitfalls.

The pride test—Everyone faces the pride test at some point, revealing the inward heart. Pride also precedes a fall from grace. So it's a top priority to teach your child the consequences of pride and how to avoid its temptations. Gifted children may also be given what is considered an Achilles heel or slight imperfection to keep them from being prideful. The apostle Paul spoke of a constant thorn assigned to him to keep him grounded because of his giftings (2 Corinthians 12:7). This thorn was to bring equilibrium to the apostle's life and counteract the potential for him to be lifted in pride.

The narcissism test—This test asks, *Does everything have to be about you?* Gifted children must learn to live alongside other children who are gifted as they are, as well as with those who have different gifts and talents. While they're young, you must teach them that each child is special whatever their gifts. In the long run, this will save you from becoming the parent of an adult narcissist. (If you have more than one child, ensure they all feel equally loved and have the same level of attention from you.)

The jealousy test—Also known as the green-eyed monster, jealousy uses fear to make us want what another person has and perhaps obsess to the point of doing anything to get it. Teach your child that "God does not show favoritism" (Romans 2:11 NIV), and they can have what God desires for them.

The greed test—Remember how Satan tempted Jesus with worldly treasures? He resisted. Teach your child Christ's example and how the apostle Paul counseled his protégé Timothy to "pursue righteousness, godliness, faith, love, endurance and gentleness" (1 Timothy 6:11 NIV) instead of succumbing to greed's pull.

The rejection test—One of the cons of being gifted is facing rejection because of your gift. Your gifted child may experience rejection from their peers because they stand out and may not fit in. It's essential to teach them how to navigate through rejection at an early age. Teach your child that they're chosen by God, separated to be used of Him, and that feeling rejected will not last forever.

The manipulation test—Kids quickly learn how to get what they want. Everyone is tested in this area regardless of giftings, but those with special gifts can be presented with the opportunity to use them to their advantage. Note that manipulation can be found in those with narcissistic tendencies. Teach your child how to avoid this pitfall and use the influence given to them appropriately.

The humility test—This test challenges one's ability to remain grounded when the opportunity arises to boast or puff up because of achievements. Note that humbleness is challenged by pride and arrogance. Kids can learn about staying grounded early as well. Parents, teach your child how to be grateful and thank God for His blessings and goodness.

Spiritual-Life Balance Assessment

The Spiritual-Life Balance Assessment worksheet in this chapter was developed from my personal experiences while raising my sons, nieces, and nephew. The following examples help explain why I chose the four categories, Spiritual, Education, Recreation, and Other. I'm sure you'll have your own examples of how life operates for you and your child in these areas.

Spiritual—On weekends we were quite busy with church services, and midweek we attended Bible study. Family prayer and word studies were informal and periodic, but we held them every Saturday and Thursday.

Education—When my sons were young and out of school for the summer, I took them to the local public library to check out books. They could choose what books they wanted, but they had to write a book report after reading them. The book reports sometimes included an oral presentation with a Q&A session at the end. I asked questions like these: *What are your takeaways? Who were the main characters?* and *What was the setting?*

Recreation—My sons played outdoors as most kids do— climbing trees, riding bikes, exploring nature, playing basketball or tennis. They were very active. Vacations were rare, but we did on occasion travel to visit relatives for the holidays.

Other—What can you think of that may not fit in the categories listed? You can place those descriptions here.

SPIRITUAL-LIFE BALANCE ASSESSMENT WORKSHEET

CATEGORY	DESCRIPTION	TIME SPENT WEEKLY	COMMENTS
Spiritual (prayer, reading, church attendance, etc.)			
Education (school, reading, workshop, labs, etc.)			
Recreation (sports, hobbies, vacation, etc.)			
Other			

Focusing on priorities, learning to manage expectations, understanding potential pitfalls and tests, and bringing balance to the lives of our prophetic children and ourselves have all been discussed in this chapter. This will help you provide support to your prophetic kids. We were also reminded to allow our kids to choose their interests while not compromising requirements, all to establish and maintain equilibrium—balance—in their lives.

PROPHETIC ACTIVITY

Complete the Spiritual-Life Balance Assessment worksheet in this chapter, for your child, yourself, or both.

- If you're completing the worksheet for yourself, substitute "work" for "education"—unless, of course, you're in school and working at the same time. In that case you can use the "other" category to record your additional data. Reviewing the four areas provided, determine where you or your child is spending the most time.
- Determine if any adjustments are necessary to bring more harmony to your lives overall.

8

Living and Leaving
a Prophetic Legacy

Some families focus on building generational wealth, and that's good. Yet what a great honor it is to also build a generational legacy through spiritual giftings that can pass down from one generation to the next. When this occurs, spiritual legacy is preserved. But when spiritual legacy is not preserved, spiritual giftings in families can become extinct and cause the next generation to fail to recognize and embrace any giftings activated in the previous generations.

So what is legacy? As defined in *Merriam-Webster's*, it's "something transmitted by or received from an ancestor or predecessor or from the past."[1] That something can be tangible or intangible. I value the intangible gifts passed down to me more than I value money. You can't, for example, buy compassion or artistic abilities, and you can't buy prophetic giftings.

How are we supposed to keep our legacy alive and functioning? The key is active preservation. We must ensure that spiritual gifts we've identified in our families are active in our children and grandchildren by teaching them how essential it is to understand and preserve the gifts, sharing stories with them from the past, and training them to activate their gifts and repeat the same process with their kids. We'll discuss this in more detail further in the chapter.

How do you know if people in your family have the same prophetic gifts someone in the previous generations had? Family gatherings are a great place to talk to older relatives and learn about past relatives and their giftings. They may share story details that only they know and give insight into family traits and commonalities.

Although I thought I was very different from others as a child, I later learned that my prophetic gifts are generational. Although my mother and her mother may not have realized it, they were seers, as are my aunts, sister, and many of my cousins. God showed them events before they happened, just like He did with me.

For the longest time, I didn't understand my prophetic gifts or how to operate within them. But as I learned their purpose and how to sharpen them, I was certain I would teach my children about their own giftings and how to embrace them. I would also teach them how to properly use their gifts, because this is part of my living out a prophetic legacy. Prophetic gifts come with great responsibility, and nothing is worse than a gift improperly used.

The Proper Use of Prophetic Gifts

Let's use the gift of seeing to explore the kind of teaching your prophetic child must receive from you and any mentor they have. You'll see a few cautions and strategies I shared earlier in the book, but I believe they bear repeating on this topic.

Seek God's wisdom and instruction

The gift of seeing can be startling to the person who's seeing into the future—especially for a prophetic child. The seer can see good and bad, and once it's seen, it can never be unseen. It can be haunting to see a tragic event before it happens, and usually the only thing you can do about it is pray and warn others as God instructs.

When God shows a seer something disturbing ahead of time, they must seek Him for wisdom and instruction for how to handle the information. They must ask questions like these:

- Is what I've just seen for me personally, or for someone else?
- Is it for the body of Christ?
- Does it involve national security for my country?
- Does it involve national security for another country?

The answers to these kinds of questions depend on many factors, which can open the door for even more questions. But seers must not look for those answers from anyone but the Lord.

Seek God's guidance for follow-through

Once their questions have been answered, seers must ask God, *What do I do with what I've seen?* For example, they can't just call up the president of the United States and say, "This is what God showed me." They'd be deemed insane. But they can ask God how to disseminate the information if it's to be shared. His answer may be to keep it in prayer and perhaps to share it with other intercessors for them to pray about it as well, both in hopes that the event will be somehow avoided or its impact lessened.

Seers must also keep what God shares with them as pure as possible. They should spend considerable time in prayer to root out any potential contamination to the prophetic word, dream, or vision. They should never be impulsive and eager to share something they're unsure of. It's better to wait for full confirmation from God than to blurt something half-cocked. They must also weed out their human nature and personal opinions.

Seek God's help in standing firm

Sometimes a seer will feel like maybe they haven't heard or seen what they actually know they have. They can't base their prophetic gift on emotion, though. They are a child of God not led by their soul but by the Spirit.

Seers run the risk of scrutiny anytime they publicly share what God has shown them in private. What happens if what they've seen doesn't come to pass—if they miss it? They can be labeled a false prophet and their words viewed as not credible. They must be careful to seek God for the assurance of what He shares with them and then stand firm.

As I've shared before, God's word will always be confirmed—if He said it, it will come to pass. There's no need to dispute over it or defend it. God's word will speak for itself. And God will teach your child to trust Him even in their prophetic gifts.

Generational Blessings

Money, real estate, and other personal assets are normally the focus when thinking about generational blessings. Saving and building wealth to leave your children and grandchildren is good planning. Proverbs 13:22 says, "Good people leave an inheritance to their grandchildren" (NLT). And according to one article, family inheritance is "the passing on of material property from one generation to another."[2]

An inheritance, however, is anything of value passed down to children and grandchildren. Sometimes what families inherit is intangibly valuable, such as a good name or notable character-istics like compassion and kindness. Conceptual and documen-tary photographer Anna Ream studies the eyes of her subjects and explains that intangible inheritance focuses on "the transfer of values and personality traits from one generation to the next."[3] When those inherited "values, traits and behavior pat-terns" intertwine with a child's character traits, that child can be impacted negatively or positively.

UNESCO (the United Nations Educational, Scientific and Cultural Organization) describes intangible inheritance as intangible cultural heritage, "traditions or living expres-sions" passed from one generation to the next. These living expressions may consist of knowledge in how to achieve in an area or certain skills passed down, like farming or artistic abilities.[4]

In Hebrew culture, a tremendously important intangible blessing is passed down from one generation to the next, usu-ally with the firstborn receiving the greater blessing, as we see in the Bible with Jacob and his sons and grandsons. The He-brew word for blessing is *berakah*, which comes from the root *barak*, meaning "to be . . . adored."[5] Many blessings or prayers are noted in the Old Testament and are still active in Jewish tradition today; the children of Israel used to recite blessings over loved ones, friends, and for special occasions. It's with great honor, however, that an elder called the family together to release the blessing before dying. Jacob did so with his family.

As Jacob's earthly transition drew near, he followed tradi-tion and called in his sons to leave a blessing on each one. A generation before it was Isaac transferring the blessing to Jacob, and before that it was his grandfather, Abraham, blessing his father, Isaac. Jacob proceeded to prophesy over them as well as Joseph's two sons. Jacob was so moved by Jo-seph's sons that he included them in the blessing. They would receive an inheritance along with their father, Joseph, and their uncles.

Although this custom is noted in the Old Testament, it can still be beneficial today. The blessing is usually given by the patriarch of the family, but it can also be given by the matriarch. As believers, if we follow the pattern, we, too, can pass on the blessing to our seed and so on, creating the generational blessing for our bloodline.

My maternal grandmother was the matriarch of our family, and she gave several family members specific instructions the day before and the day of her passing. "This will be my last time seeing you. I'm going away," she said as she walked out the front door of my house that early Sunday morning.

I discerned she was giving hints about her earthly transition, but I had no idea it would occur the very next day. She knew she would be transitioning soon, shared the news with us, and wanted to make sure she spoke with each member of the family she needed to. Sure enough, the following Monday afternoon we got the news that she was gone, just as she foretold. She may not have left millions of dollars, but she left her wisdom and prophetic gifts passed down to my mom, then to me and my children.

These are some examples of generational blessings:

- a repeated pattern of long life from generation to generation
- birthing many happy and healthy children
- material wealth passed from one generation to the next
- good education with most graduating high school and college
- long marriages
- little to no divorce from generation to generation
- two-parent homes

Generational Curses

Generational curses may counteract any positive impact on a generation, so you need to be aware of what the enemy will attempt to attach to your bloodline. A generational curse is an attack from the enemy repeated from generation to generation, based on any wrong actions your relatives may have taken.

But it may also be the result of their rebellion against God. The book of Psalms speaks to this:

> Do not hold against us the sins of past generations; may your mercy come quickly to meet us, for we are in desperate need. Help us, God our Savior, for the glory of your name; deliver us and forgive our sins for your name's sake.
>
> Psalm 79:8–9 NIV

Look for the patterns

Look for the patterns in your bloodline to understand what attacks the enemy may have used against you and your family. Once you trace the types of attack, you can begin to intercede on behalf of your family and also teach your child about generational curses and how to break them. Be sure to trace both lines, maternal and paternal.

These are some examples of generational curses:

- a repeated pattern of premature death from generation to generation
- barrenness or sterility in the women or men of the family
- poverty from one generation to the next
- poor education where most do not graduate high school
- early childbearing
- widespread divorces
- single-parent homes

Break the curses

You can break generational curses by committing yourself to God and being an intercessor, standing on behalf of your family through prayers and prophetic decrees that align with what you need to see manifest rather than the negative patterns you traced. According to Romans 4:17, we can call into being what does not yet exist.

Declarations you can speak to break generational curses:

I take authority over premature deaths in my bloodline.

I take authority over sickness and disease.

I decree and declare long and healthy lives in my bloodline.

I take authority over barrenness and sterility in the women or men of the family.

I decree and declare open wombs, healthy full-term pregnancies, and healthy births.

I take authority over the spirit of poverty and financial struggles from one generation to the next.

I decree and declare wealth, financial wholeness, and wisdom to steward finances well from generation to generation.

I take authority over any early childbearing before adulthood.

I take authority over widespread divorces in my bloodline.

I decree and declare long and healthy marriages in my bloodline.

I take authority over poor education and barriers to high school and college graduations.

I decree and declare that my children, grandchildren, nieces, nephews, and cousins will graduate high school and college and lead successful careers.

Philip's Prophetic Legacy

Philip of the Bible and his four daughters are a great example of gifts passed down to the next generation.

Philip is one of the disciples Jesus handpicked to follow Him during His visit to Galilee. Philip found his friend Nathanael and shared that he'd met the one Moses spoke of in the law books and the one the prophets prophesied about. The Bethsaida native followed Jesus and was an eyewitness to all the healings and miracles that occurred through Him.

Philip was there both times Jesus performed the miracle of multiplication. Philip was the one Jesus asked how much money they had, knowing they didn't have enough to feed five thousand men plus women and children.

> He was testing Philip, for he already knew what he was going to do. Philip replied, "Even if we worked for months, we wouldn't have enough money to feed them!" . . . "Tell everyone to sit down," Jesus said. So they all sat down on the grassy slopes. (The men alone numbered about 5,000.)
>
> John 6:6–7, 10 NLT

Philip was also part of the great commission released to Christ's disciples when He proclaimed to them that power was coming through the person of the Holy Spirit and that the gospel would spread through them throughout the earth: "You will receive power when the Holy Spirit comes upon you, and you will be My witnesses in Jerusalem, and in all Judaea and Samaria, and to the ends of the earth" (Acts 1:8).

The great commission didn't necessarily occur peacefully. The New Testament church was scattered after the altercation and murder of Stephen, who was stoned to death by those opposing the message of Christ. However, instead of being afraid to share what they'd experienced with Christ, the disciples boldly spread the gospel everywhere. Philip, ordained a deacon, became an evangelist who traveled and preached the gospel, and he started his traveling ministry in Samaria:

> Philip went down to a city in Samaria and proclaimed the Christ to them. The crowds gave their undivided attention to Philip's message and to the signs they saw him perform. With loud shrieks, unclean spirits came out of many who were possessed, and many of the paralyzed and lame were healed.
>
> Acts 8:5–7

At some point, Philip's four daughters, who aren't named in the Bible, were introduced to Christ and the ministry where the gifts of the Spirit were in operation. Philip's entire family probably moved with him when the church was scattered. His daughters no doubt saw and heard of the miraculous events in the Samaritan city. The gifts of the Spirit in Philip were passed down to his daughters, who all had the gift of prophecy—foretelling the future.

Their prophetic gifts are confirmed by the apostle Paul in Acts 21:8–9: "Leaving the next day, we reached Caesarea and stayed at the house of Philip the evangelist, one of the Seven. He had four unmarried daughters who prophesied."

Just as God used Philip and his daughters, He can use you and your child. Very recently, I learned something new from my aunt. Back in 1987, before my grandmother passed away, she told my aunt about a virus coming that would kill a lot of people. The scientific community would not know what it was, she said, but they would give it a name. My aunt didn't share this with others until the advent of COVID-19. Who knew the entire world would be shaken by a plague-like sickness that would shut down nations?

My youngest son, a proven prophetic voice, saw the virus five years before it happened. He wrote a book about it as well as many other things happening now. What he saw about the virus was precise: doctors would first think the virus was the flu because the symptoms were so similar.

Understanding and Preserving Legacy Gifts

The main key to the preservation of gifts from one generation to the next is knowing and understanding what gifts existed and have already been passed down. The apostle Paul identified the gift of faith in Timothy, his mother, and his grandmother: "I am reminded of your sincere faith, a faith that dwelt first in your grandmother Lois and your mother Eunice and now, I am sure, dwells in you as well" (2 Timothy 1:5 ESV).

All too often generational gifts are overlooked because they haven't been identified as such. After learning about spiritual gifts as a young believer, I was encouraged to identify what gifts I had, even those in seed form. Dreams are certainly evident in my life. As a young girl, I heard older family members discussing a dream they had, but I never connected the dots telling me that being a dreamer was generational.

Although my mother didn't understand prophetic gifts, she was a vivid dreamer too. And one dream saved her life. She was having health issues, but doctors couldn't find anything wrong.

Then in a dream God showed her what the medical issue was, and she went into the hospital just in time for emergency surgery. Had she waited until the next day, she would have died. Paying attention to that dream allowed my mother to see her children and grandchildren grow up.

In this chapter we've learned about teaching children the importance of prophetic gifts and how to properly use them, generational curses and blessings, and how to understand and preserve generational gifts. The following prophetic activity will help you with the latter task before we move on to the process of letting go.

PROPHETIC ACTIVITY

Assess the spiritual gifts passed down to you and your child. You may need to talk to family members about what they remember about those who've passed on. A chat with your elders in particular could reveal the answers you need.

Here is a Legacy Gift chart that includes some of the more common gifts. Use it to record what you learn, adding to it any more unusual gift you find in your family. Then share this information with your child to help them understand and appreciate generational blessings, especially any their own family enjoys.

LEGACY GIFT CHART

Gift	Description	You	Child(ren)	Maternal Side	Paternal Side	Notes
Discerning of spirits	Divine ability to distinguish between good and evil					
Word of Wisdom	Divine ability to instruct how to do something					
Word of Knowledge	Divine ability to know information without being told beforehand					
Gift of Prophecy	Divine ability to foretell a future event					
Prophetic Dreams	Divine ability to see a future event while asleep					
Prophetic Visions	Divine ability to see a future event while awake					
Gifts of Healing	Divine ability to heal the sick					

Letting Go

Raising children with four distinct personalities has truly been a journey for me. I remember when my sons didn't want to wear identical outfits anymore. Yes, I was that mom, but they soon developed their own taste and style. My oldest went through the FUBU everything-matching phase—hat, shoes, shirt, and jeans.

As they came into their own styles naturally, they also developed their own spiritual giftings. With keen spiritual eyesight, they often shared with me things God had shown them while in prayer or in a dream related to the church or an individual. Some of the revelations were warnings from God to beware of upcoming disparaging situations or events. If one of them came to me with a warning dream, I asked about every detail, knowing that even the most minute ones can be critical when attempting to interpret a dream.

Our assignment as parents shifts when our kids move into adulthood, but it never stops. We move from being needed daily to that of a consultant on an as-needed basis. After building a foundation for our child, assisting in the development of their prophetic gifts, and exhibiting and helping them create spiritual-life balance, we must allow them to grow and mature independently.

As the mother of four adult sons, my position as parent is more of an advisory role now. They may bounce something off me when they think a discussion is needed, and I always try to be available when they need me. But for the most part, my job is to watch from the sidelines and cheer them on as they build and live their lives.

Let's tackle how and when to step back.

Maturity for Parents

Most parents think about maturity in relation to their kids, but maturity is also required of the parents—allowing their child's proper development and then knowing when to let go at each stage. Yes, we have to let our kids grow up and go through the process required to move from child, to preteen, to teen, to adult.

At times, we might believe we know our kids better than they know themselves and refuse—or at least hesitate—to give them the opportunity to grow and evolve into who God wants them to be. Yes, we may know their personality and tendencies from childhood, but we may not know who they will be as adults. They need to become more and more independent, and too much parental control along the way can cause challenging or even irreversible damage to their development.

Of course, supervision is still necessary, but with each phase comes a different level of governing. For instance, we wouldn't allow a five year old to be home alone after school as we would a child who's in middle or high school. Of course, like others, I was a latchkey kid. But times have changed. Afterschool programs are available now. But you get the point. You're more apt to allow your teenager to be alone in the house after school than you would your elementary-age child. The level of governing is different.

And yet parents tend to think of their kids as the babies, toddlers, and adolescents they were instead of who they're becoming as adults. But to think like this only adds to the desire and sometimes need to control the life of the precious one whose total existence was once their responsibility. Most parents only want what's best for their children, but there can be a thin line between wanting what's best and control. It's kind of like that thin line between sanity and insanity or between love and hate. We just can't stand not controlling it—"it" being the very life we brought into this world.

You've spent your child's life laying a foundation suitable for moral living, using real-time situations as teachable moments, and guiding them down the path they should take. But after all is said and done, you have to exit the driver's seat so they can sit there instead, place their own hands on the steering wheel, and be in charge of their own way in life.

The Dos and Don'ts of Letting Go

You've taught your child the basics. You've laid the foundation. Now it's time to let them implement everything you've poured into them. But you must learn to adhere to dos and don'ts.

Here are six things to remember during the letting-go process:

1. *It's imperative that you don't run interference in major situations and events in your child's life.* This is true even if you sense they may not be making the wisest decision. Sometimes what we're sensing is correct, but we may go about addressing it the wrong way to get our point across or share our opinion. Interference can produce confusion and in turn disrupt the harmony of the parent and adult child relationship.

2. *Don't get mad or upset if your child makes a choice totally opposite from the one you advised them to make.* You raised your child to be an independent thinker, and now you must let them think. Critical thinking is part of the growth process. If they make choices that aren't the best, they'll learn to correct their mistakes through trial and error just like you—and we all—did and still do. (Come to think of it, if you didn't listen to everything your parents advised you to do either, history may be on repeat. It sounds familiar, doesn't it?) Of course, it can be challenging when you think they're about to make the wrong decision in an area, but you have to come to the place where you realize they must walk the process themselves as you stand on the sidelines and coach.

3. *Support your child's decisions.* Your support is needed even if you don't agree with your child's decisions. For example, your son or daughter may decide to start a new life in a different state or even in another country. But because you want them to be near you, you might be tempted to try to control the narrative by making up excuses for why they shouldn't go. But when you don't support your child's decisions, you're sending a message that you don't support them. That's how they'll perceive it. Ask yourself if the decision makes them happy (them, not you). Here are some areas where you can support your adult son or daughter rather than trying to control them:

- what college or university they choose to attend or the trade they choose to train for
- the career they choose to pursue
- where they choose to live
- whom they choose to date
- whom they choose to marry

4. *Step in only because of imminent danger or because your child asked you to.* Don't take back the wheel unless you're asked to and it really is the wisest thing to do. And even if you see imminent danger ahead, proceed with extreme caution so as not to damage your child's confidence.

5. *Never condemn your child for making a mistake.* Provide constructive feedback, but don't tear them down. Instead, help put them back on a more positive path by building them up, showing them where they may not have made the best decision, and assisting them in finding a solution they agree with.

6. *Be there to catch your child when they fall.* When things don't happen the way your adult child thought they would, save your "I told you so." Again, they'll make mistakes just as we did and still do. You can't "mistake proof" their life. Mistakes are a part of learning how to navigate through life. But be there to catch them when they fall. They still need a support system. Don't throw them to the wolves; the world cares nothing about them.

Praying for Your Adult Child

I still pray for and cover my sons, asking God to protect and keep them, let His will be done in their lives, and establish and expand them.

When should you pray for your child? Both when they need you and when they don't need you. Pray when the Holy Spirit moves you to pray for them. Pray for them when you see a pitfall ahead or see or sense something is wrong. Pray for them when you see they're unhappy or bothered by something.

And how do you pray for them? Sometimes in my quiet time, I whisper prayers for my sons. At other times I pray loud and boisterously when I think it's needed. I pray like my life depends on it. I stand between heaven and earth with liquid intercession, praying that God will move, that things will go right, that things will turn around, that things will be successful, that favor will be released. That's how I pray. During these intense moments, I may not be able to share with my sons what or how I'm praying, but I think they're aware and can sense when I'm in this type of prayer mode. They're spiritually sensitive and can feel the prayers.

The length of time you spend in prayer regarding a specific situation depends on the urgency of the need. Some prayers are short with immediate results, while others aren't answered for months or even years. But you are your child's greatest intercessor. Many lives have been changed because of parents' prayers. Don't be afraid to let the devil know he cannot have your child.

Here is a prayer of guidance for your adult son or daughter:

Father, my prayer is that . . .
   You will lead my child to the right path to take for their life.
   You will not allow them to detour from the path you have set for them.
   You will send them help when needed.
   You will show them who is to walk that path with them.

Here is a prayer regarding relationships for your adult son or daughter:

Father, I pray that . . .
   My child will seek to know you and serve you all their life.
   They will cross paths with those who will have a positive influence in their life.

They will discern those with ill motives seeking their friendship.
They will appreciate those you have placed in their life.
They will seek out a godly mate who is grounded in you.
They will have patience with those you place in their life.

And here is a prayer of success for your adult son or daughter:

Father, my prayer is that . . .
My child will be established on the earth.
They will have favor with you and with man.
They will achieve their goals in life.
You will make their way prosperous.
You will use them for your glory.

Using the following prayer point chart as an example, identify specific topics you want to cover on behalf of your adult child. Then create prayer points and find Scriptures to support them as you implement them into your times of prayer. These examples address some of the more difficult challenges your child could be facing, not only in adulthood but in adolescence prior to adulthood.

PRAYER POINT CHART

Topic	Prayer Point	Supporting Scripture
Feeling Unloved	God has accepted you as His beloved.	To the praise of the glory of His grace, by which He made us accepted in the Beloved. (Ephesians 1:6 NKJV)
Depression	The joy of the Lord is your strength.	Don't be dejected and sad, for the joy of the Lord is your strength! (Nehemiah 8:10 NLT)

Topic	Prayer Point	Supporting Scripture
Low Self-Esteem	Lift up your head.	Lift up your heads, you gates; be lifted up, you ancient doors, that the King of glory may come in. (Psalm 24:7 NIV)
Loneliness	God is always with you. You have nothing to fear or be discouraged about.	The LORD himself goes before you and will be with you; he will never leave you nor forsake you. Do not be afraid; do not be discouraged. (Deuteronomy 31:8 NIV)
Fear	God has not given you the spirit of fear. I take authority over the spirit of fear in your life.	God has not given us a spirit of fear, but of power, love, and self-control. (2 Timothy 1:7)
Suicidal Thoughts	You will live and not die.	I will not die, but I will live and proclaim what the LORD has done. (Psalm 118:17)
Harmful Habits/ Addictions	God has given you power over the enemy to break every habit and addiction.	The weapons of our warfare are not the weapons of the world. Instead, they have divine power to demolish strongholds. We tear down arguments and every presumption set up against the knowledge of God; and we take captive every thought to make it obedient to Christ. (2 Corinthians 10:4–5)
Mental Illness	God transforms your mind.	Do not be conformed to this world, but be transformed by the renewing of your mind. Then you will be able to test and approve what is the good, pleasing, and perfect will of God. (Romans 12:2)
Unhealthy Soul Ties	You have authority to break the power of darkness off your life. You have healthy boundaries and relationships.	I have given you authority to tread on snakes and scorpions, and over all the power of the enemy, and nothing will hurt you. (Luke 10:19 ESV)

Serious Challenges Your Child May Face into Adulthood

If your prophetic child experiences some of the challenges in this example prayer point chart as an adult, it may be even more challenging for you to let go because of the additional support they'll likely need. That support could even be an extension of the support you gave them during their earlier years.

One study found that "for almost 50 percent of patients, mental disorders start before they reach adulthood, highlighting the importance of early intervention and prevention measures for mental health issues in adolescents."[3] So supporting your child in a journey of mental illness, for example, may be an integral part of your ongoing relationship and reliance on God's grace and strength.

Whether your child faces any of these challenges in adulthood or before, your prayers and support as their parent are key to their ability to thrive. Let's look more closely at four of the possible challenges, starting with mental illness.

Mental illness

The enemy likes to attack the mind with bombarding thoughts, released in a barrage of unacceptable arguments to make one doubt being loved, capable, or enough. Trauma is often a gateway to mental injuries and triggers, and the injured mind must receive inner healing to get better.

Some illnesses may be due to chemical imbalance, a disorder, or a disease that plagues the mind. Medication or surgical procedures may be required. If it's been determined that no medical issues are causing the mental attacks, spiritual deliverance may need to occur.

Another way to combat mental attacks is to focus on positive thoughts by meditating on the Word of God and dispelling anything negative that tries to invade the mind. Medical

News Today calls this "mindfulness" and says, "Mindfulness practices involve regulating thoughts, feelings, and behaviors."[1] A comparable strategy is found in Philippians 4:8: "Fix your thoughts on what is true, and honorable, and right, and pure, and lovely, and admirable. Think about things that are excellent and worthy of praise" (NLT).

Harmful habits or addictions

Galatians 5:1 tells us, "Stand fast therefore in the liberty by which Christ has made us free, and do not be entangled again with a yoke of bondage" (NKJV). Ungodly habits and addictions are tied to spiritual bondage and need to be addressed in prayer for the person to be delivered. Deliverance from some habits and addictions also requires fasting along with prayer. Once liberation from the habit or addiction takes place, it's important for the person to refrain from being around those who are still enjoying what bound them.

It was previously thought that it takes only twenty-one days to break a habit, the same number of days to form one. But a recent scientific study concluded that both "habit formation and breaking can take anywhere between 18 to 254 days."[2] Regardless of the time medical science deems for a habit to be broken, the power of prayer can make a difference in making lifestyle changes.

Unhealthy soul ties

Before discussing unhealthy soul ties and how to break them, let's talk about healthy soul ties. Examples include Jonathan and David, who the Bible describes as so close that their souls were knit together. They were covenant brothers. First Samuel 18:3 says, "Jonathan swore eternal friendship with David because of his deep affection for him" (GNT). Jonathan even warned David about his father King Saul's evil plans, and it saved David's life.

A soul tie occurs when two souls knit together, whether through friendship or a romantic relationship. This can happen when intimate information or personal feelings are shared with another individual often. Soul ties occur over time as the individuals become closer, bonding through commonalities, whether spiritual or natural. If healthy boundaries are not in place, the connection has the potential to evolve into an unhealthy relationship.

Soul ties can be placed in four categories:

1. spiritual—connecting on a spiritual level
2. physical—connecting through physical intimacy
3. emotional—connecting on an emotional level
4. social—connecting through a social bond

Later, when David became king, he honored his covenant with Jonathan by restoring honor to his lineage and sparing the life of Mephibosheth, Jonathan's son, bringing him to live in the palace to be treated like the prince he was: "The king spared Mephibosheth son of Jonathan, the son of Saul, because of the oath before the LORD between David and Jonathan son of Saul" (2 Samuel 21:7).

Someone may have an unhealthy soul tie if they're so obsessed with another person that they can't function without seeing or hearing from them, they're extremely upset if the other person doesn't immediately return their call or text, or when they know a relationship has turned toxic but it's difficult to leave it.

Unhealthy soul ties can even turn dangerous. Someone can feel as though they're unsafe in the presence of the other person due to their unpredictable behavior. The controller may even say they love them, but fearing violence will occur if the potential victim attempts to leave is an indication of toxicity in the relationship. At some point, the person must recognize that toxicity and do whatever it takes to break the soul tie.

Suicidal thoughts and self-harm

Strong urges to harm one's self and constant thoughts of death and dying are demonic attacks against the mind, body, and soul. The enemy knows if these strong urges are carried out, death could result, thus robbing the person of a potentially fulfilled life. Most who battle with suicidal thoughts and thoughts about harming themselves have experienced major trauma at least once. The enemy takes advantage of the pain associated with the trauma and makes them feel that if they end it all, the pain will stop.

If your child faces any of these or other serious challenges as a young child, or teen, or certainly as an adult, your roles as advisor and cheerleader while maintaining prayer support are all the more crucial.

Restoring Communication with Your Adult Child

When the opportunity to talk with your child actually ceases, you feel it to your core. Their anguish is your anguish, although they may not experience the same crushing impact the situation has on you. Fathers will suffer with such a separation as well, but as a mom, there's no way you can carry a precious soul for nine months, be one with the rhythm of that child's heartbeat, and not be disturbed when that rhythm is disconnected.

Mom, if you adopted your son or daughter, that process didn't connect you with your child as it would have in the womb. But you still experienced the oneness and rhythm of two heartbeats through the bonding process. You, too, will wonder, *What could I have done differently?* Sometimes nothing. Each soul must find their own way.

If it's not obvious, ask God to show you the root cause of the broken communication between you and your child so it can be repaired. Perhaps the circumstances were less than ideal surrounding your child's conception or birth, and so the disconnect actually began in the womb or in the days following birth. Or perhaps unconscious thoughts hindered proper bonding between you and your child, the footprint for building good communication.

Perhaps many years have passed since you were able to really sit down and talk candidly, but don't let the passing of time be an excuse for not attempting to restore the lines of communication. And if you do have the right opportunity to talk, ask God to move in the moment and bring restoration to the relationship. Remember, your child is your legacy. Don't miss opportunities to build your legacy.

When asking God for a healthy relationship with your adult child, remember these five important truths:

1. *Healing takes place over time.* Don't rush the process. You may need to wait until things cool down to talk. You may also need to set aside your pride and be the first to reach out.

2. *Harsh words can sabotage unity.* Harsh words are not easily forgotten, so be careful what you say and how you say it. "Seek to understand, then be understood," a quote by Stephen R. Covey, makes a great point.

3. *It's crucial to actively listen to what your child is saying.* When the lines of communication do open, be willing to really listen to what your child has to say. Also pay close attention to their body language as they speak, because emotional gestures are language too. And don't listen to react but to understand. If we only want to have a conversation to get our point across or

make someone understand what we're saying, we've missed it. If we want our adult children to hear us, we have to first be willing to hear them and make their feelings valid. James 1:19 says, "Everyone should be quick to listen, slow to speak, and slow to anger." Following this biblical suggestion could speed up the healing process.

4. *Don't tell your child how they feel; let them tell you.* But remember, people sometimes leave, run away, or distance themselves when they feel unwanted or unloved. If your child expresses such feelings, ask God to reveal the truth to you and guide you on how to address what your child has shared.

5. *It's not about who's right and who's wrong.* Don't open old wounds by bringing up the past, as they can be triggers that cause your child to shut down and distance themselves again. Let go of old grudges about what you thought you heard them say and how they may have treated you. Let your child have the moment. And again, you may need to set aside your pride and be the first to reach out. But do so with caution, not attempting to justify why you feel the way you do. We parents tend to do that—justify our actions. Let your child be free to become who God has purposed them to be, and continue to pray and strive for a healthy relationship. But the process may mean growth on your part as well as on theirs.

Praying for Your Unsaved Adult Child

It's not easy to watch your adult child detour from the teachings you've poured into them from childhood. But if that occurs, you can only take the stance of prayer. This is quite difficult and painful, because the first thing you want to do is run to their rescue. But you can't. You can only be there to listen, love, and support.

Here is a prayer for your unsaved adult son or daughter:

> *Father, my prayer is that . . .*
> *My child will accept you as Lord and Savior.*
> *They will live a life pleasing to you.*
> *They will walk in your ways.*
> *You will lead and guide them into all truth.*
> *You will direct their path.*

In this chapter, we've come to terms with what it may take to effectively support our children when they become adults. First Peter 2:5 in *The Message* paraphrase of the Bible says, "Present yourselves as building stones for the construction of a sanctuary vibrant with life, in which you'll serve as holy priests offering Christ-approved lives up to God." We're all living stones on this journey called life. Some are smooth. Some are rough. Some are jagged. Yet we are all the same. Be patient and kind with your child, and extend the same grace you desire to be extended to you.

May God set you, a parent, in place as a stone of honor that sits on display in brilliance and divine illumination to shine greatly, impacting the world and embracing your purpose.

PROPHETIC ACTIVITY

Formulate a strategy to pray for your adult child. And pray for what they need, not just what you desire.

- Ask God for insight as you put together words that bring life, encourage success, and remove barriers that block destiny and cause derailment of purpose.
- Identify any challenges your adult child is encountering.
- If applicable, choose a topic from the prayer point chart to integrate it in your prayers for your adult child.
- Incorporate supporting Scriptures as you pray.

CONCLUSION

Let's review and summarize some of the key truths, strategies, and building blocks I've shared to help you achieve raising prophetic kids to be all God intends them to be.

Stewarding Your Prophetic Child

As their parent, you can steward your child from conception to adulthood by

- creating a spiritually rich environment for them
- speaking life over them at each stage
- laying a critical foundation of prayer and God's Word to assist them in understanding and embracing their purpose
- gaining knowledge of and breaking generational curses in the bloodline on their behalf
- speaking declarations that release positive words over their life for every situation

Naming Your Prophetic Child

The birth of a child is exciting, and so is their naming. The meaning of your child's name is best well thought out before you permanently assign it since they'll live with it for a lifetime. In biblical times, names were given to children based on events, whether good or tragic. If the event was tragic, the name may not have been in the child's best interest. The name Jabez is an example in the Scriptures. Jabez refused to be satisfied with the meaning of his name—"I gave birth to him in pain." So he asked God to free him from the impact of what that name represented as well as to bless and expand his life.

This example shows how you can ask God to reverse what has been negatively spoken over you and your child.

Developing Your Prophetic Child's Gifts

I believe every child is born with seeds of greatness inside them, and they need parental guidance to unlock the power of those seeds so they can develop into what they're meant to be. Here are things to remember in their development:

- *When prophetic gifts are fostered in young children, the chance of their operating in those gifts at an earlier age is greatly increased.* Such was the case for my four sons, who at a young age were taught about their prophetic gifts, which were consistently nurtured. In turn, activation was inevitable. Having insight into the prophetic dimension provided guidance for how to assist my kids on the path to their destiny. My prayer is that you, too, will have this help in raising a prophetic kid.
- *The more your child knows about their gifts and how to develop them, the easier it will be for them to exercise them.* For instance, if they're a dreamer, you can

help them create and use a dream journal. This can be a time for you to bond, make memories, and teach them about the types of dreams they're having.

- *The development of seeds takes time.* What may start out as unshapely and unrecognizable can grow into beautiful gifts identifiable by you and others. But you must allot the proper time for them to grow.

- *The seeds must be fertilized to become visible.* And once they are, you must keep watering them until seedlings appear and can be nurtured to grow into a tree that bears the fruit of its kind. Each seed will take on their own distinction and function as intended.

- *To enhance the development of your child's prophetic gifts, build a proper prophetic foundation by instituting prayer in the home and teaching them how to establish their own personal prayer life.* If there is resistance in these areas, ask God to show you how to pray for them and to give you wisdom on how and when to speak to them about it. Continue to include them in family prayer times.

- *As your child's gifts grow and develop from seed form, they will be more easily identified.* This is the case whether they come in the form of dreams, visions, or any one of the nine spiritual gifts categorized under the three main groups: power gifts, speaking gifts, or mind gifts.

Acknowledging the Supernatural in Your Prophetic Child's Life

Supernatural encounters do occur. The spirit world is real, and prophetic kids will often have supernatural experiences. These can be divine encounters, or they can be nightmares or ungodly experiences.

You can prepare your child by teaching them two things: (1) how to tell the difference between a divine encounter and an ungodly experience, and (2) how to take authority during demonic encounters by using the name of Jesus to dispel those entities.

Providing Mentorship for Your Prophetic Child

When your child is ready to embrace and understand their gifts, it may be best to bring a mentor into the picture, someone who has experience in the prophetic gifts they're developing. Search out a mentor trustworthy for both you and your child to provide guidance and support.

Achieving Spiritual-Life Balance for Your Prophetic Child

The spiritually gifted often struggle to strike a balance between living a normal life and being overwhelmed by their gifts. Using the Spiritual-Life Balance Assessment worksheet in this book breaks down how much time is spent in each of several areas. This can help both you and your child adjust where needed so as not to experience burnout due to imbalances in life. If spiritual abilities are properly balanced, they're more apt to be preserved and embraced in the next generation.

Preserving Your Prophetic Legacy

It's a great honor for you when your adult child teaches their own kids what you taught them, embracing and developing their prophetic gifts because they understand the importance of perpetuation from generation to generation. When this happens, preservation of the legacy continues.

Families may have prophetic gifts that are multigenerational, but if the importance of preserving those gifts is not understood, they may become extinct. Researching the blood-line, talking to older relatives, and discussing prophetic gifts regularly at family gatherings keeps the knowledge of those gifts alive from generation to generation.

Knowing When and How to Let Go

In families where prophetic gifts flourish and kids are allowed to grow and develop their gifts at a young age, the time comes when parents have to step back and watch their children mature in their prophetic gifts. While used to managing your child's life, you must now take on the roles of coach and advisor as they become an adult, cheering them on from the sidelines. But be ready to step in and assist at a moment's notice, praying and speaking declarations over their life just as when they were a kid.

The birth of a child comes with many responsibilities. How-ever, watching your child grow and develop in their purpose is a beautiful thing, knowing they're being nurtured with godly influence. The journey will be most adventurous with many twists and turns along the way, but not to worry. With God's help and by applying the tools in this book, you can do this.

But don't sweat the small stuff. Kids need to know it's okay if they spill the milk every now and again, miss a curfew, or dent the car. Love them unconditionally, and they'll be better for it.

As parents, we're not perfect; we will make mistakes along the way. But if we lead with love, our children will reflect on the tough times and realize we exhibited love through them. And for those of us who now have adult children, let's keep our posture of prayer from the sidelines, stepping in when needed as they walk through this journey called life.

May God bless you as you raise and support your prophetic child.

ACKNOWLEDGMENTS

To God—Thank you for allowing me to birth and steward such precious souls as my sons and for teaching me how to nurture each one and help develop their prophetic gifts.

To my four sons, Tevin, Torien, Tarris, and Joshua—You have been my driving force to write and share the contents of this book with the world. Its concepts have been forged through your training and development in the prophetic. It has been an honor to be your mother and watch you become the men you are today.

To my granddaughter, Londyn—You already know you carry a great legacy. I love your sweet spirit, determination, and love for God. And I love that your parents have taught you many of the concepts in this book they learned and how you apply them in your own life.

To my daughter-in-love, Renale—You have become a great prayer warrior and daughter, and I love your tenacity for the things of God. It's an honor to be your mother-in-love.

To my nieces and nephews—I hope the small part I played in your upbringing watered the seeds of greatness in you, causing you to blossom into the beautiful flowers you're becoming.

To my family—Thank you for your ongoing love and support. May we continue to preserve the legacy of prophetic gifts passed down through generations by teaching them to our children and grandchildren.

To my special friend Linda—You encouraged me to write and watched me blossom over the years. Thank you for believing in me, listening to me sharing my dreams, the gentle nudging, and always supporting me on my many projects.

To my core group, Chelsea Gardner, Jacquie Cheek, and Lynne Thomas, to name a few—You have allowed me to mentor you several times over, taking every class I've offered even after already taking them two or three times—because you didn't want to miss learning something new. Thank you for supporting every project I've launched over the last two decades.

To my friends Prophetess Runette Jones, Apostle Phyllis Morton, and Carla Alston—Thank you for your prayers and support for so many years.

To my late parents, Johnnie Mae and Lawrence Thomas—Thank you for allowing me to be a self-starter, an independent thinker, and to pursue my dreams. I wish you were here to see how much the seeds you planted have bloomed.

To my literary agency, Embolden Media Group—Thank you for your hard work and dedication in helping me get this book published.

To my publishers, Baker Publishing Group and Chosen Books—Thank you to the team for bringing this book to life, for the opportunity to share my voice as a writer, and for making this a wonderful experience.

NOTES

Chapter 1 Cultivating a Spiritually Rich Environment

1. Jessica Timmons, "When Can a Fetus Hear?" Healthline, January 5, 2018, https://www.healthline.com/health/pregnancy/when-can-a-fetus-hear.

2. Shawn Manaher, "Decree vs Declare: The Main Differences and When to Use Them," The Content Authority, accessed October 6, 2023, https://thecontentauthority.com/blog/decree-vs-declare.

3. *Merriam-Webster's Collegiate Dictionary*, s.v. "gift," accessed October 9, 2023, https://unabridged.merriam-webster.com/collegiate/gift.

4. Rishi Sriram, "Why Ages 2–7 Matter So Much for Brain Development," Edutopia, June 24, 2020, https://www.edutopia.org/article/why-ages-2-7-matter-so-much-brain-development.

5. Sriram, "Why Ages 2–7 Matter So Much."

Chapter 2 Becoming Your Child's Destiny Helper

1. Jamie Friedlander, "10 Ways Your Name Affects Your Life," *Success*, March 11, 2016, https://www.success.com/10-ways-your-name-affects-your-life.

2. Christian Jarrett, "How Your Name Affects Your Personality," BBC, May 25, 2021, https://www.bbc.com/future/article/20210525-how-your-name-affects-your-personality.

3. Frank T. McAndrew, "Why the Choice of Your Child's Name Matters So Much," *Psychology Today*, October 5, 2020, https://www.psychologytoday.com/us/blog/out-the-ooze/202010/why-the-choice-your-childs-name-matters-so-much.

4. "Why Do I Need a 'Hebrew Name'?," Chabad.org, accessed October 6, 2023, https://www.chabad.org/library/article_cdo/aid/80495/jewish/Why-Do-I-Need-a-Hebrew-Name.htm.

5. Cleveland Kent Evans, "Cultural and Ethnic Influences on Baby Names," How Stuff Works, June 13, 2006, https://lifestyle.howstuffworks.com/family/parenting/babies/baby-name-trends-ga2.htm.

6. Zushe Wilhelm, "How and When a Girl Is Named," Chabad.org, accessed October 6, 2023, https://www.chabad.org/library/article_cdo/aid/273284/jewish/3-How-and-When-a-Girl-Is-to-Be-Named.htm.

7. Evans, "Cultural and Ethnic Influences on Baby Names."

8. Mia Sogoba, "The Power of a Name," Cultures of West Africa, February 11, 2019, https://www.culturesofwestafrica.com/power-of-names/.

9. Team Baby Gogo, Naming Traditions: "How to Name Babies in India," Baby Gogo, accessed May 9, 2023, https://www.babygogo.in/naming-traditions/.

10. Nicolas Cabrera, "Dos Apellidos: When Families Have Two Surnames," Denver Public Library, November 17, 2020, https://history.denverlibrary.org/news/genealogy/dos-apellidos-when-families-have-two-surnames.

11. McAndrew, "Why the Choice of Your Child's Name Matters So Much."

12. *Merriam-Webster's Collegiate Dictionary*, s.v. "develop," accessed October 9, 2023, https://unabridged.merriam-webster.com/collegiate/develop.

13. *Merriam-Webster.com Dictionary*, s.v. "destiny," accessed October 6, 2023, https://www.merriam-webster.com/dictionary/destiny.

14. *Merriam-Webster.com Thesaurus*, s.v. "destiny," accessed October 6, 2023, https://www.merriam-webster.com/thesaurus/destiny.

15. *Merriam-Webster.com Dictionary*, s.v. "effort," accessed October 6, 2023, https://www.merriam-webster.com/dictionary/effort.

Chapter 3 Building a Prophetic Foundation

1. Balogun Kamilu Lekan, "Queen Elizabeth II: Biography, Education, Ascension, Coronation, Reign, Achievements, Husband, Children, Net Worth, Controversy, and More," News Wire NGR, September 8, 2022, https://newswirengr.com/2022/09/08/queen-elizabeth-ii-biography-education-ascension-coronation-reign-and-achievements-husband-children-net-worth-controversy-and-more.

2. "Queen Elizabeth II," History.com, updated April 25, 2003, https://www.history.com/topics/european-history/queen-elizabeth.

3. Shlomo Riskin, "Parshat Toldot: Brothers, Birthrights and Blessings," *Jerusalem Post*, November 23, 2006, https://www.jpost.com/jewish-world/judaism/parshat-toldot-brothers-birthrights-and-blessings.

4. *Merriam-Webster.com Dictionary*, s.v. "construct," accessed October 6, 2023, https://www.merriam-webster.com/dictionary/construct.

5. "Who Is Eli in the Bible?" Got Questions Ministries, accessed October 6, 2023, https://www.gotquestions.org/Eli-in-the-Bible.html.

6. Nissan Mindel, "Eli the High Priest," Chabad.org, accessed October 6, 2023, https://www.chabad.org/library/article_cdo/aid/112391/jewish/Eli-The-High-Priest.htm.

7. I learned these categories years ago from Kenneth E. Hagin, *The Holy Spirit and His Gifts* (Tulsa, OK: Kenneth Hagin Ministries, 1991), n.p.

8. "Comparison of Fruits of the Spirit & Gifts of the Spirit," The Holy Spirit, accessed October 6, 2023, https://theholyspirit.com/study-series/the_9_gifts/.

Chapter 4 Activating Your Child's Prophetic Gift

1. "Hebrew Letter Charts," Hebrew Resources, accessed October 6, 2023, https://hebrewresources.com/hebrew-letter-charts.

2. Cornelius Kant, "The Feast of Shavu'ot," Christians for Israel International, June 7, 2019, https://www.c4israel.org/_teachings/the-feast-of-shavuot/.

3. *The American Heritage Dictionary of the English Language*, s.v. "warning," accessed October 6, 2023, https://www.ahdictionary.com/word/search.html?q=warning.

4. *Strong's Concordance*, s.v. "4394. prophéteia," Bible Hub, accessed October 6, 2023, https://biblehub.com/greek/4394.htm.

5. *Strong's Concordance*, s.v. "4253. pro" and "5346. phémi," Bible Hub, accessed October 6, 2023, https://biblehub.com/greek/4253.htm and https://biblehub.com/greek/5346.htm.

Chapter 5 Acknowledging Your Child's Spiritual Experiences

1. "Nightmare Disorders," Mayo Clinic, https://www.mayoclinic.org/diseases-conditions/nightmare-disorder/symptoms-causes/syc-20353515.

2. Beth Roybal, "Sleep Paralysis," WebMD, April 8, 2023, https://www.webmd.com/sleep-disorders/sleep-paralysis.

3. Jennifer Atwater, "Protecting Children's Ears, Eyes, and Hearts," 911 Life, accessed May 9, 2023, https://www.911life.org/protecting-childrens-minds-ears-eyes-and-hearts.

4. "God Looks at the Heart," Got Questions Ministries, accessed May 9, 2023, https://www.gotquestions.org/God-looks-at-the-heart.html.

5. Jessica Van Roekel, "3 Essential Questions to Guide What Your Kids Watch and Listen To," Crosswalk.com, February 15, 2022, https://www.crosswalk.com/family/parenting/essential-questions-to-guide-what-your-kids-watch-and-listen-to.html.

6. The Britannica Dictionary, s.v. "authority," accessed October 6, 2023, https://www.britannica.com/dictionary/authority.

7. "7 Facts About Your Authority as a Believer," Kenneth Copeland Ministries, June 7, 2022, https://blog.kcm.org/7-facts-about-your-authority-as-a-believer.

Chapter 6 Understanding the Power of Mentorship

1. Lorne A. Adrain, comp., *The Most Important Thing I Know: Life Lessons from Colin Powell, Stephen Covey, Maya Angelou, and Over 75 Other Eminent Individuals* (New York: MJF Books, 1997), 60–61.

Chapter 7 Teaching Balance for Lifelong Prophetic Service

1. Quizlet, s.v. "balance," accessed October 9, 2023, https://quizlet.com/512223827/balance-flash-cards.

2. Sporcle, s.v. "balance," accessed October 9, 2023, https://www.sporcle.com/reference/answer/balance.

3. "The 7 Habits of Highly Effective People," FranklinCovey, accessed May 9, 2023, https://resources.franklincovey.com/mkt-7hv1/the-7-habits-of-highly-effective-people.

4. "Habit 3: Put First Things First," FranklinCovey, accessed May 9, 2023, https://www.franklincovey.com/habit-3.

5. Linda Stade, "Help Your Kids Create Balance and Calm in Their Lives," September 28, 2021, https://lindastade.com/helping-kids-create-balance-in-life.

Chapter 8 Living and Leaving a Prophetic Legacy

1. *Merriam-Webster's Collegiate Dictionary*, s.v. "legacy," accessed October 9, 2023, https://unabridged.merriam-webster.com/collegiate/legacy.

2. Liliana Sousa, Ana Raquel Silva, Liliana Santos, and Marta Patrão, "The Family Inheritance Process: Motivations and Patterns of Interaction," *European Journal of Ageing* 7, no. 1 (March 2010), https://www.ncbi.nlm.nih.gov/pmc/articles/PMC5547277.

3. Anna Ream, "Intangible Inheritance," accessed May 9, 2023, http://www.annaream.com/portfolio/intangible-inheritance.

4. "What Is Intangible Cultural Heritage?," UNESCO, accessed May 9, 2023, https://ich.unesco.org/en/what-is-intangible-heritage-00003.

5. *Brown-Driver-Briggs Hebrew and English Lexicon*, s.v. "bless," accessed October 9, 2023, https://biblehub.com/hebrew/1288.htm.

Chapter 9 Letting Go

1. Emily Cronkleton, "Mindfulness and Emotional Well-Being Strategies," Medical News Today, February 25, 2022, https://www.medicalnewstoday.com/articles/mindfulness-for-mental-wellbeing.

2. Suzy Davenport, "How Long Does It Take to Break a Habit and What Is the Best Way to Do It?" Medical News Today, October 11, 2022, https://www.medicalnewstoday.com/articles/how-long-does-it-take-to-break-a-habit.

3. Sebastian Ocklenburg, "At What Age Does Mental Illness Begin?," *Psychology Today*, June 18, 2021, https://www.psychologytoday.com/us/blog/the-asymmetric-brain/202106/what-age-does-mental-illness-begin.

Founder of both FaithNation and Debra Giles Ministries, an online ministry equipping social media platforms, **Debra Giles** is a workshop facilitator, conference speaker, teacher, and preacher. She has served in various five-fold ministerial functions, including more than twenty years as a lead pastor before relocating to Minneapolis, Minnesota.

Debra is part of the Mantle Network, an apostolic and prophetic ministry that supports five-fold leaders through education, training, and spiritual covering. She is also under the covering of the AIM family, founded by Dr. I. V. Hilliard, and she ministers across both the United States and Europe.

Debra has a bachelor's and master's degree in business administration. Her vast career has spanned across multiple industries, including program management and supplier diversity in government contracting, legal assistance for large corporations, commercial and family law firms, and floral design and entrepreneurship.

She uses her corporate skills and experiences to mentor those wanting to grow spiritually and navigate life's challenges. She also helps entrepreneurs develop strategies to grow their businesses.

For more information about Debra, see the information below.

DebraGiles.com

DebraThomasGiles

DebraGilesMinistries